Anonymous

Official Reports of Battles

Embracing Col. Wm. L. Jackson's report of expedition to Beverly; Maj. Gen. Price's report of evacuation of Little Rock; Maj. Gen. Stevenson's report of battle of Lookout Mountain. Vol. 4

Anonymous

Official Reports of Battles

Embracing Col. Wm. L. Jackson's report of expedition to Beverly; Maj. Gen. Price's report of evacuation of Little Rock; Maj. Gen. Stevenson's report of battle of Lookout Mountain. Vol. 4

ISBN/EAN: 9783337325367

Printed in Europe, USA, Canada, Australia, Japan

Cover: Foto ©ninafisch / pixelio.de

More available books at **www.hansebooks.com**

REPORTS OF BATTLES;

EMBRACING

COLONEL WM. L JACKSON'S REPORT OF EXPEDITION TO BEVERLY; MAJOR GENERAL PRICE'S REPORT OF EVACUATION OF LITTLE ROCK; MAJOR GENERAL STEVENSON'S REPORT OF BATTLE OF LOOKOUT MOUNTAIN; AND LIEUTENANT COLONEL M A. HAYNES' REPORTS OF ENGAGEMENTS AT KNOXVILLE, LIMESTONE CREEK AND CARTER'S STATION.

PUBLISHED BY ORDER OF CONGRESS.

RICHMOND:
R. M. SMITH, PUBLIC PRINTER.
1864.

MESSAGE OF THE PRESIDENT.

RICHMOND, VA., Feb. 15, 1864.

To the Senate and House of Representatives:

I herewith transmit, for your information, communications from the Secretary of War, covering copies of several additional reports of military operations.

JEFFERSON DAVIS.

COMMUNICATION FROM SECRETARY OF WAR.

CONFEDERATE STATES OF AMERICA,
War Department,
Richmond, Va., Feb. 12, 1864.

To the President of the Confederate States:

SIR: I have the honor to forward, for the information of Congress, copies of the following reports:

Colonel William L. Jackson, and subordinate commanders, of expedition to Beverly.

Major General Sterling Price and Colonel Dobbins, of evacuation of Little Rock.

I am, sir, very respectfully, your obedient servant,

JAMES A. SEDDON,
Secretary of War.

COMMUNICATION FROM SECRETARY OF WAR.

CONFEDERATE STATES OF AMERICA,
War Department,
Richmond, Va., Feb. 13, 1864.

To the President of the Confederate States:

SIR: I have the honor to forward, for the information of Congress, copies of the reports of Major General Stevenson and his subordinates, of the battle of Chattanooga, and Lieutenant Colonel M. A. Haynes, of engagements at Knoxville, Limestone Creek and Carter's Station.

I am, sir, very respectfully, your obedient servant,

JAMES A. SEDDON,
Secretary of War.

REPORT OF COLONEL WM. L. JACKSON.

HEADQUARTERS NEAR HUNTERSVILLE,
July 11, 1863.

To Major CHARLES S. STRINGFELLOW,
    A. A. General, Southwestern Department of Va.:

MAJOR: I have the honor to submit, herewith, the proceedings of the expedition to Beverly:

On Monday, the 29th ultimo, the force under my command moved as follows: Detachment of cavalry, under command of Captain John S. Spriggs, moved from Clover Lick to Big Spring; detachment of cavalry, under command of Captain J. W. Marshall, was advanced from a point near Green bank to Clover Lick; the infantry at this camp, accompanied by a section of artillery, commanded by Lieutenant F. G. Thrasher, of Chapman's battery, moved to within five miles of Big Spring; Captain John Righter, with his company of cavalry and parts of Campbell's, Arnett's and Evans' companies, moved on to the Staunton and Parkersburg turnpike, through what is known as the Cheat Pass; Lieutenant Colonel A. C. Dunn, with detachment of his battalion and Captain E. M. Corder's company, accompanied by several excellent guides, on the same day moved from Hightown to a short distance beyond Slaven's Cabin, when he took a route to the right, leading to the rear of Beverly on the Phillippi road.

On Tuesday evening, the 30th ultimo, the infantry, artillery and the detachments of cavalry, under Captains Marshall and Spriggs, encamped a few miles beyond Valley mountain.

On Wednesday evening, the 1st instant, Major J. B. Lady was ordered, with two companies which he has raised under authority of the Secretary of War, and parts of three other companies of my command, to proceed to the rear of Beverly, on the road leading to Buckhannon. He turned to the left about two miles and a half beyond the Crouch fortifications, and, by blind paths through the woods, succeeded, by his own indomitable energy, the assistance of his guides, and the patient perseverance of his men, in reaching the position.

He was ordered to close upon the enemy whenever he heard my artillery. How he performed his duty will be seen by the report herewith submitted. I am of the opinion, that, unaided as he was, in the attack hereafter mentioned to have been made by Lieutenant Colonel A. C. Dunn, he (Major Lady) accomplished all that he could under the circumstances. I omitted to mention that I sent, to support Major Lady in his rear, Sergeant Rader, with twenty mounted men, to Middleford Creek bridge, eighteen miles in his rear. They performed their duty faithfully.

On Thursday morning, at daybreak, I reached Huttonsville, and found that Captain Righter, who had written instructions as to the position of the pickets of the enemy to within five miles of Beverly, and orders to capture them, permitting none to escape, was engaged in executing his orders. He had surrounded the pickets at each post, and captured all, fourteen in number. Ascertaining the time when the relief pickets would arrive, and that I had time to spare, under the arrangement with Major Lady and Lieutenant Colonel Dunn, I sent forward Captain Marshall, with a portion of his company, and he, in connection with Captain Righter, so posted the men as to surround a certain position when the relief came. The relief arrived in time, fourteen in number, and they were all captured. The road was now clear to within a mile and a half of Beverly, and the surprise would have been complete, had it not been for a woman, who, in some way, discovered our approach, and who met a party of about twenty-five of the enemy, including the colonel commanding at Beverly, taking a morning ride, unconscious of our proximity.

Within eight miles of the place I moved about two hundred men, including the company of Captain George Downs, commanded by Lieutenant William Harris; Captain J. W. Ball's company, commanded by Lieutenant C. W. Minter, (Captains Down and Ball being absent, sick;) parts of Young's and Lewis' companies, under Lieut. R. D. Lurty; Captain S. H. Campbell's company; some recruits, not organized, under Sergeant E. Tibb's, and some mounted men, under Captain John M Burn, all under command of Major D. B. Stewart, across the Valley river, on the Back road, so as to get on the right flank of the enemy, and to be in position to co-operate with or support Lieutenant Colonel Dunn, if he advanced. Major Stewart performed the duty assigned him entirely to my satisfaction, and gives, in his report, an account of his operations, a copy of which is herewith enclosed.

I then moved to the front of Beverly, throwing forward the detachment under Captain Spriggs, to the Burnt bridge, which was the centre of my operations in front, Major Stewart being on the right, and the detachment under Captain Marshall to the left, on the Back road, leading to the Buckhannon road. A considerable force of the enemy advanced on this road; but were promptly driven back by Captain Marshall, assisted by a flank movement of Captain Spriggs.

Such was the disposition of my force, that the enemy were entirely surrounded, if Lieutenant Colonel Dunn was in position, and he had ample time and competent guides. The force of the enemy did not exceed one thousand, including infantry, cavalry and artillery, of which they had four pieces. My force exceeded theirs by at least two hundred, including that under Colonel Dunn. At two o'clock, P. M., I ordered my artillery to open, which was the signal for the general attack to be made.

From my position, having a clear view of the field, I saw no movement on the part of Lieutenant Colonel Dunn. I then had my artillery supported by Captain Neal, with his and parts of two other companies, (Captain Marshall also being in a position to support,) placed in position on a hill opposite the position of the enemy, about one mile distant, and then commenced an "artillery duel" (hoping that time would be given to Lieutenant Colonel Dunn to come up and take part,) in which the enemy had the advantage of position, number of pieces, and quality of ammunition. Not more than one in fifteen of our shells exploded. No material damage was inflicted or incurred. One howitzer was slightly disabled by a piece of shell, but was soon soon repaired. The enemy occupied a very strong position on Butcher's hill, in the rear of the town, near the Phillipi road. I felt confident in the ability of my force, without the assistance of that under Lieutenant Colonel Dunn, to drive them from that position, but as my object was to capture, not to run them, I delayed the assault, yet hoping to hear from and to see Lieutenant Colonel Dunn; but he was not to be found.

During the night I ordered Major Stewart back a short distance to a safe position, holding the ground I had obtained during the day in the front. Early the next morning, (the 3rd instant,) having heard nothing from Lieutenant Colonel Dunn, I determined to assault the position of the enemy. Accordingly, I ordered Major Stewart up to the position he held the evening before. In advancing to do so, the skirmish, referred to in his report, occurred. I dismounted a considerable portion of my cavalry, and was moving to the assault, when I discovered a reinforcement coming to the enemy on the Phillippi road, and was also advised of the same by Major Lady and Captain Marshall. My own opinion is, that the reinforcement received numbered at least seven hundred; others, and prisoners, estimate it at a greater number. I saw about seven hundred mounted men entering the place.

Having now become satisfied that if Lieutenant Colonel Dunn ever reached the position to which he was ordered, he had fallen back, and that it was imprudent to continue the attack, I made demonstrations in front for four hours, in the mean time drawing in the forces under the command of Majors Stewart and Lady, and sending scouts to communicate with Lieutenant Colonel Dunn.

At two o'clock, P. M., of Friday, the 3rd instant, I slowly retired in a manner to prevent my being flanked, or the enemy reaching my rear. The enemy did not follow me on that day, and about nine o'clock, P. M., I went into camp at the crouch fortifications with my infantry and artillery, posting my cavalry between that point and Huttonsville.

It is proper now to state that Major J. R. Claiborne with a detachment of one hundred mounted men of Dunn's battalion, who, on the way, was ordered to follow me, (which order, left at Warm Springs, he did not receive, and without it was coming up to reinforce me,) was met, as I was falling back, about six miles this side of Beverly. I left him in the rear during Friday night, as his men and horses were comparatively fresh.

In the morning (the 4th instant,) I received dispatch number one, from Lieutenant Colonel Dunn, a copy of which and copies of dispatches numbers two and three, are herewith enclosed. I immediately ordered Major Claiborne to cross the river at the point he then was, some four miles from Huttonsville, and more to a point near Stripes', towards the Cheat Pass, and to communicate with Lieutenant Colonel Dunn, who was supposed to be coming that way. I ordered the detachments, under Captains Marshall and Spriggs, to Huttonsville, to cover this movement of Major Claiborne, and masked my artillery and infantry about one mile this side of the Crouch fortifications. The force at Huttonsville was directed to fall back towards me in good order, if any considerable advance was made by the enemy on the route I was taking, and Major Claiborne or Lieutenant Colonel Dunn, if he came up to Stripes', was, in the event of such advance, to come in upon the rear of the enemy, while I would attack them in front. If there was no such advance by two o'clock, P. M., then Major Claiborne or Lieutenant Colonel Dunn was to fall back towards Hightown, and the detachments at Huttonsville to fall back to me. Major Claiborne reached the point near Stripes' and dispatched to Lieutenant Colonel Dunn; but it now appears that he had fallen back to camp Bartow, and was not advancing.

A short distance beyond Huttonsville, soon after the arrival of the detachments there, Captain Spriggs, being in front, had a skirmish with the advance of the enemy, they falling back with a view, no doubt, to draw him to their main force; but, as ordered, Captains Spriggs and Marshall fell back a short distance, and there awaited a further advance. While this was going on, Major Claiborne so manoeuvred as to disconcert the enemy, as was evident by the hesitation and caution displayed. They did not anticipate the appearance of any force at the point where he was, and could not comprehend its strength.

Advised of this advance, I moved my infantry and artillery back to the Crouch fortifications, directing the several detachments of cavalry to fall back slowly towards my position. This order was executed, the enemy advancing when the cavalry receded, and halting and hesitating whenever they halted and formed line of battle. A junction being formed of the three detachments aforesaid, Major Claiborne, by my order, took command of all my cavalry. The pursuing force numbered about eighteen hundred.

Ascertaining that the enemy would not advance on my position, or risk a general engagement, and that the waters were rising rapidly in my rear, I fell back with the main command to Marshall's store, and encamped there during the night, the cavalry encamping a few miles in my rear. While this movement was being accomplished, the enemy fell back to Beverly. Lieutenant Colonel A. C. Dunn, it appears from his own dispatches, was in position at the time appointed. He was ordered to make a vigorous attack upon the rear of the enemy whenever he heard my signal. This it was impossible for him to avoid hearing. I am reliably informed, that instead of advancing and attacking as ordered, he fell back when my signal was heard. His dispatches are contradictory in the attempt to explain this singular retrograde movement. I have felt it my duty to order him under arrest, and will prefer charges. Major J. R. Claiborne is now in command of the battalion.

Our loss in the attack and various skirmishes is as follows:

Killed four; wounded five, and missing four. Among the killed was the gallant Lieutenant Wm. Harris, who died after being mortally wounded, while bravely leading his men in a brilliant charge.

The loss of the enemy, from the best information I can obtain, is as follows:

Killed forty; wounded sixty seven; prisoners fifty five.

We also captured a number of horses, cavalry equipments and arms. These I will send you a list of, and ask what disposition shall be made of the horses as soon as I can get the necessary reports, which, owing to the disposition of my force, rendered necessary to carry out my orders, are delayed.

The officers and men of my command, with but few exceptions, performed their duty faithfully and cheerfully throughout the whole expedition notwithstanding it rained every day but one, and the mud and deep waters through which they were compelled to wade. I regret that the limits of this report will not admit of honorable mention of all who exhibited personal bravery and high soldierly qualities.

I am compelled, however, to bear testimony to the distinguished conduct of Captains Spriggs. Marshall, Righter, and Elihu Hutton, and Lieutenant Thrasher, of the artillery, and Lieutenant Jacob W. Wamsly. I was much indebted throughout to Captain Marshall on account of his thorough knowledge of the country, personal bravery and excellent judgment.

Accompanying this report is a rough and somewhat imperfect plot of the country, the various routes taken, and the prominent points, which will give a general idea of my movements.

Very respectfully, your obedient servant,
WM. L. JACKSON,
Colonel nineteenth Regiment Virginia cavalry.

LIEUTENANT COLONEL DUNN TO COLONEL JACKSON.

HEADQUARTERS THIRTY-SEVENTH BATTALION,
Camp Tilghman, Hightown, July 9, 1863.

Colonel WM. L. JACKSON:

COLONEL: Your communication of the 4th instant was handed me by Major Claiborne on yesterday. I am now in position at Hightown, carrying out my orders from you, I having a company at Monterey, which company are picketing and scouting as far as Franklin, in Pendleton county. I am diligently scouting, and I shall fight the enemy if ever they should advance. I have sent to Staunton for twenty days' rations for my command. I am sorry our plans were not successful in capturing the enemy. I was in my position two hours before the time given by you, and have done everything in my power to carry out your orders, and, in fact, have done more than you ordered me to do. Mr. Caplinger, one of my guides, left, near Beverly, on Tuesday. He says the enemy reinforced some two thousand five hundred men, and on Friday morning, shortly after, I fell back. They advanced and secured the position I held, thinking I was still there. They could not find out how I got in their rear or how I went out. He says the reinforcements had left for Grafton, leaving Colonel Harris' forces still in Beverly.

I am, Colonel, your obedient servant,

A. C. DUNN,
Lieutenant Colonel commanding.

I certify this to be a true copy.
W. S. LURTY, *Adj't 19th Va. Cavalry.*

REPORT OF MAJOR LADY.

HEADQUARTERS LADY'S BATTALION,
Camp Northwest, July 11, 1863.

W. L. JACKSON,
   Colonel Commanding :

SIR : In compliance with your orders of the 28th ultimo, at half-past four, P. M., I proceeded to the rear of the enemy on the Buckhannon road, with five companies, commanded by the following officers: Captains Evans, Arnett, Hayhurst, Duncan, and Lieutenant Boggs, making a total, rank and file, one hundred and fifty strong. After a forced march of twelve miles, over a series of the most rugged and pathless ridges of a densely timbered mountain section of country, fording streams, &c., I reached the base of Rich mountain at three o'clock, A. M, of the 29th ultimo. The men being exhausted and unable to advance without rest, I halted two hours. At the command "halt," the men dropped from their feet and slept till five o'clock, A. M., when, at the command "fall in," though weary and foot-sore, they cheerfully and promptly responded, and I proceeded as far as Armstrong's cabin, near the summit of the mountain, where I allowed the men to wash and fill their canteens. Here Mr. Armstrong proffered his services to open a road, as the brush was so thick as to render it almost impossible to pass through between this point and the road, at which point I arrived at ten o'clock, A. M., being five miles west of Beverly. I halted my men near, but concealed from, the road, where they were shaded and in reach of pure water. I immediately threw forward a picket of twenty men, under command of Lieutenant Hunt, with orders to proceed carefully, without causing alarm, to within two miles of Beverly, and take a concealed position commanding the road, where he would be enabled to notify me of the movements of the enemy and cut off all communication on the road, and at the first report of artillery to move forward and "cut off" the enemy's picket. I also sent a courier to notify Colonel Dunn of my position and my readiness to co-operate with him in any movement on the town. At one o'clock Lieutenant Hunt sent in two prisoners, who were going home on furloughs granted by Colonel Harris, commanding the enemy's forces, whose statements corresponded with your previous information, except in reference to the reinforcement expected that day. I remained in this position till three o'clock, P. M., when the "signal gun" was fired, when I immediately ordered my men in line of march and moved rapidly forward to within a mile and a quarter of town, taking a position which I could have held against any force the enemy could have brought from town. This position was at the first abrupt turn in the road west of the Baker house. I then sent forward Captain Arnett to take a concealed position in front, sweeping the road and commanding the only position on which the enemy could have posted artillery, without first driving him back with an infantry force, to have done which, would have brought them under fire of the reserve of my command on their left flank. I at the same time sent forward Captain Evans, with a squad, to reconnoitre between me and the town and examine the fortifications near the Baker house. In an hour he reported that the enemy had evidently determined to make a stand in town and that a strong position could be taken beyond the Baker house, near the old breastworks. I moved forward my command as far as practicable without bringing it in range of the enemy's artillery, and halting the command, I went forward and examined the ground in front and fully approved the position selected by Captain Evans. I then moved my men forward to a strip of woods, near where I had first halted them and allowed them to remain there till I could move them under cover of night to the position selected. About this time the cavalry scout reported to me that they had carried out all their instructions, besides finding the notorious Yankee spy and bushwhacker, Simmons, in his own house. On demanding of him a surrender, he peremptorily refused, and commenced firing, killing private Dent, of ——— company, a gallant soldier, whereupon our men returned the fire, killing him, four balls passing through his body. I immediately ordered them to endeavor to open communication with Colonel Dunn, which, up to that time, I had been unable to do, having had no mounted men with me, and my dismounted men being too much fatgued to attempt it. I placed Captain Evans, with forty men, on the road to blockade and picket the same, and open the engagement should the enemy advance or evacuate the town. I at the same time posted Capt. Arnett, with his company, on the adjacent height to support Captain Evans, reserving the companies of Captains Hayhurst, Duncan, and Lieutenant Boggs, under my command. We remained in this position till the morning of the 30th. At about eight o'clock the cavalry reported that they had not been able to open communication with Colonel Dunn. An hour after this time, and while the cavalry were grazing their horses, the front of the enemy's reinforcement, which I estimated at seven hundred strong, appeared on the Phillippi road, advancing rapidly in the direction of Beverly and getting within a mile of my position. I sent a squad of cavalry to reconnoitre and ascertain more definitely their number and report their movements. I at the same time dispatched a courier notifying you of this reinforcement. At about half-past nine, A. M., from the movements of the enemy's infantry, cavalry, and artillery, I was assured that they intended turning a force on me for the purpose of cutting off my retreat. One piece of their artillery being so placed as to sweep the road on my line of retreat, and deeming it inexpedient unnecessarily expose my men, I fell back to the position first described, on entering the road so as to protect them from the range of artillery, allowing Lieut. Clancy to remain to notify the squad of cavalry of the change, and ordering them, through him, to report to me forthwith on their return from their reconnoitre. While in this position, your first dispatch came to me, ordering me to "fall back and join you immediately, and should the enemy attack me to fight him and fall back," which I had already prepared to do. I had sent Lieutenant Poe forward, with a squad of ten men, as an advanced guard, and Captain Duncan, with ten men, back, as a rear guard, to notify me of the enemy's approach from either direction. From this point and in this order I joined you without any interruption whatever.

My thanks are due to the officers and men under my command for the patience and endurance exhibited on this fatiguing expedition, and for the prompt manner in which they responded to all calls made upon them. And I am especially indebted to Captains Evans and Arnett for their valuable assistance in selecting positions and the skillful handling of their men.

Respectfully, your obedient servant,
JOHN B. LADY,
Major commanding detachment.

REPORT OF MAJOR STEWART.

CAMP NORTHWEST, *July* 9, 1863.

Colonel W. L. JACKSON,
Commanding Huntersville Line:

SIR: I herewith transmit the following report of the part taken by me and the troops I had the honor to command during the late investment of Beverly, in Randolph county, Virginia:

After leaving you below Huttonsville, on the morning of the 2nd instant, we moved forward as directed on the Back road, as fast as the condition of the men would permit; received a dispatch from Captain Marshall, to which I replied, as I dispatched to you from Mr. Wamsley's. As I had information from the front that was entirely satisfactory, I depended entirely on my cavalry scouting the road till some two miles above Henry Harper's, where I detached Captain Campbell's company, and ordered it to deploy on my right as skirmishers.

I had been informed by soldiers, who reported to me at Wamsley's, that they had scouted the road from a short distance above Burnt bridge, that the enemy had no picket at Harper's house. I moved my skirmishers so as not to discover my approach to the enemy till at a point opposite Ward's, from which the position of the pickets could be determined. I here found them still in position at Harper's house, and accordingly detailed twenty-five men and sent them forward to take possession of both roads beyond their post. With them I sent my two guides, Wamsley and Currence. Shortly after they had moved forward, a courier came from below (from Beverly, perhaps,) and, on his approach, they withdrew, at a full run, in the direction of Beverly. Seeing that all chance of their capture was now at an end, I moved my infantry forward, moving my skirmisher near the road, where there were woods to conceal them, and out of sight of the road, where there were none, while I made a detour to the right with the main body. Captain Burns I left with the cavalry at Ward's, where they were concealed from below. On reaching the crest of the first ridge, of which there was a complete succession, running at right angles to the river and road, I discoved a scouting party, numbering eight, of cavalry, coming on the road from the direction of Beverly. I here directed a message to be sent to Captain Burns, informing him of their approach, which I learn he did not receive, though it was unnecessary, as he could not but discover their approach. We then moved forward so as to gain the top of the next ridge, which we did just in time to prevent the scouts being fired on by Captain Campbell, who had halted, and his men were in the act of taking aim when his scouts passed up, six in number, two having halted at Harper's. I ordered him not to fire, and as soon as I could do so without giving any alarm, moved the head of the column forward to the position occupied by Captain Campbell, reaching this just a Captain Burns opened fire on them, and ordered a charge from his position above. I moved my right down to the road with orders to fire on them in case they could not halt them. Not reaching the road in time they fired, killing three and wounding one—one having been wounded in Captain Burns' fire, and one, by having his horse shot under him, was thrown in a fence-corner and taken prisoner. The whole six were thus killed, wounded or taken prisoners. One of the killed we found to be Clay Ward, a son of the Mr. Ward at whose house we had halted. We here took three head of horses, which were brought off; one escaping, wounded, and one being so badly wounded as to be unfit for service, and one being killed; and, I presume five sabres, five Colts pistols, and five Sharpe's carbines, though they were not all reported to me. We pursued the two scouts who had halted at Harper's, but as the flanking party sent out by me had not gotten in position on the road towards the Burnt bridge, they escaped in the direction of Beverly.

As your artillery had not yet opened fire, I here halted, and ordered back my flankers, and again moved as directed by your dispatch dated one o'clock, P. M. Some delay was here caused to our movements on account of the non arrival of my scouts or flanking party from above the Burnt bridge, who had not gotten in position when my messenger arrived at the point to which they had been sent. I moved, however, as nearly as I could in the direction of the Earl hill, at twenty minutes to two o'clock, P. M., without my guides, and the road being blockaded above, I moved across the country, keeping my skirmishers well out in front and halting them at intervals. The woods being so dense they could not see each other but occasionally, we could move but slowly, and our course was not direct, on account of the difficulties already mentioned. Indeed, I was thrown almost entirely on my own resources, as Lieutenant Wamsley knew nothing but the general course. With the arrival of my guides, whom I had directed to come up, I received a dispatch from you requesting me to move so as to support Captain Marshall if he moved towards the Earl hill. I was at that time in no position to see any movements that were making on my left, and as I had not sufficient cavalry to scout the country, all I could do was to move so as to gain a point from which I could do as you directed. And at about five o'clock, P. M., I reached Fontaine Butcher's farm, on the hill immediately south of Files' or Philles' creek. Here I found myself some half a mile to the right of the Earl hill, but was enabled to get a full view of the position of the enemy on Butcher's or Callett's hill, northeast of Beverley, where he had his artillery planted. Here I sent out scouts to find out whether Captain Marshall had made the movement indicated, and also dispatched to you. I intended moving to the Earl hill after sunset. Why I did not bring on an action you know. At half-past seven o'clock, I received your dispatch ordering me to take position above Harper's, which I reached by the Back road at half-past eleven o'clock, P. M.

On the morning of the 3d instant, I moved, at fifteen minutes to seven o'clock, being compelled to delay longer than I had intended in order to find the command. And at this point I had to leave about thirty men, who were unable to march. These I ordered up to Henry Harper's to be used in case I should need them. I moved forward, sending my cavalry ahead to scout the road, and detaching an advance guard from Captain Downe's company, which I passed under the command of Lieutenant Morgan.

In this manner I was enabled to reach the point indicated by you, much sooner than I could otherwise have done, and as your order to me was imperative, I did not hesitate to move in this manner, and, indeed, I consider as it safe as any I could have adopted on such ground.

On reaching Daniel's farm, at the top of the hill, on this side of Files' creek, and where there is a road leading to the Earl hill, I detached Captain Young, with his cavalry, to scout the roads, and ordered Captain Burns forward to reconnoitre the position I had occupied on the previous evening, and moved my infantry forward in supporting distance, in case he was attacked. On consultation with Lieutenant Wamsley, (and you had requested me to give his opinions due consideration,) I agreed to move my infantry to nearly their old position, which I would not have done if I had not taken his advice, but would have placed them on the right in a wood land.

As you had dispatched to me that you were " about to dismount Sprigg's command and send them in the rear or flank of the enemy," and added, " you may come up with him or he with you," I directed scouts to be sent towards Earl hill, supposing he might come up from that point. As there was but a small skirt of woods, and part of that cut away, I deemed it safer to send but the cavalry forward, afterwards moving up the infantry, and resting in place preparatory to moving forward in line of battle, the ground having been passed over by Captain Burns.

Your artillery had now (fifteen minutes to nine o'clock, A. M.) nearly ceased playing, and no firing of small arms being heard, I wrote a dispatch to Captain Young, directing him to scout fully the road in the direction of Earl's hill. And I was on the point of sending one to you informing you where I was, etc., I was fired on by the enemy in ambush, the first fire, a single shot, striking my horse. I immediately ordered the men to " fall in," and on that order being given the fire became general along the enemy's line, which I then discovered to be an extended one, and at some forty or fifty yards distant, except a right flank, now left, as we found, for action, faced to the rear. This fire at first produced some excitement along the line, and produced a little wavering which pervaded the action till nearly its close. A simultaneous movement was immediately ordered of the whole line, and the battalion now rushed forward with deafening cheers on the position of the enemy in our immediate front, giving him a raking fire, which we were enabled to do before he could reload. A few, however, had either reserved their fire, or had gotten their arms reloaded, and gave us one fire, sharp and scattering, at which time Lieutenant William Harris, commanding Captain Downe's company, fell mortally wounded, while gallantly leading his company. The men, with few exceptions, now pressed forward, and the route of the enemy became complete. And as he was formed with a stout worm fence, staked and ridered, in his rear and on his left, and another old worm fence, grown up with underbush, on his right, leaving but a single place for his men to retreat through, so that in their attempt to retreat our men were enabled to deliver their fire with such deadly aim that fourteen of his killed and wounded were left immediately on the ground. The skirmish now became a running one, our men following and firing, the enemy retreating and not returning our fire. On the right where I now was, I saw three of the enemy fall while running through an oat field, and from the most reliable information I could get, and from a report made me by Lieutenant Lake, who afterwards examined the field, some fourteen at least of the enemy were left in different portions of the field, making in all, from thirty to thirty-five of the enemy left on the field, not including those wounded slightly.

Our loss was trifling compared with theirs, and consisted of the following: Captain Down's company, Lieutenant Wm. Harris commanding: Killed—First Lieutenant Wm. Harris; wounded—Private Richard Wine, in side slightly; Captain Bell's company, Lieutenant Minter commanding: killed—none; wounded—Privates Daniel B. May, in side badly, John S. Robertson, in arm, Leonard Radcliffe, in arm slightly; Captain Campbell's company: killed—Private Alfred Owens; wounded—Second Sergeant Henry Smith, badly; Randolph Wamsley, Captain Marshall's company, guide, wounded mortally. Killed three; wounded five.

It would afford me great pleasure to bear testimony to the several acts of gallantry performed by the several companies I commanded. I must here bear testimony to the good conduct of Lieutenant Wamsley, of Captain Marshall's company, who advanced with the first charge calling out, "come on, don't let the d—d Yankees whip us on our own soil;" to Lieutenant J. G. Gittings, my acting adjutant, who rendered me valuable assistance by bringing up the right with loud cheering, and to that of Randolph Wamsley, of Captain Marshall's company, who rushed into the fight, though acting only as a guide, but who, I am sorry to record, fell, mortally wounded. After falling back the troops, and rallying them on the ground where the skirmish took place, I had the wounded cared for, and, communicating with my cavalry command, I ordered the infantry back to a rise immediately in my rear, where I could not be flanked, and sent out a picket to occupy the ground in front of where the skirmish took place.

Here I received your dispatch ordering me to fall back to Ward's, which I immediately proceeded to do, going to the rear to attend to the wounded, and have the dead interred. The wounded I had taken to Mr. W. Daniel's, and made arrangements to have them cared for; the citizens agreeing to have the dead decently buried. In falling back to Huttonsville, I made arrangements to have all my broken down troops brought up, ordering my cavalry to dismount in order to bring them up.

As you are fully aware of the condition in which I turned over the command to you, allow me to subscribe myself,
Very respectfully, your obedient servant,
D. BOSTON STEWART, *Major, &c.*

P. S. The enemy's force, in the skirmish, on the morning of the 3d instant, as stated by his wounded, amounted to over two hundred men. Ours did not amount to more than one hundred and forty men in infantry. Our cavalry was not in the action.

Respectfully, &c.,

D. BOSTON STEWART.

REPORT OF MAJOR GENERAL PRICE.

HEADQUARTERS PRICE'S DIVISION,
Camp Bragg, Nov. 20, 1863.

Lieutenant Colonel JOHN F. BELTON,
Assistant Adjutant General, District of Arkansas:

COLONEL: I have the honor to submit the following report of the military operations which terminated on the 10th of September, in the evacuation of Little Rock by the forces then under my command.

Having been notified, on the 23rd of July, that Lieutenant General Holmes desired to relinquish his command to me, during the continuance of his severe illness, I left Des Arc, the then headquarters of my division, the same day, and, having reached Little Rock the next, assumed command of the district of Arkansas.

Being satisfied that the enemy was about to advance in heavy force upon Little Rock, I sent orders the same day to Brigadier General Frost, commanding the defences of the lower Arkansas, near Pine Bluff, to move at once, with his infantry and artillery, to Little Rock.

Orders were also sent, on that day, to Brigadier General Fagan, upon whom the command of my division (Fagan's, Parson's and McRae's brigades of infantry,) had devolved, directing him to withdraw his forces from Searcy and Des Arc and to take position upon Bayou Metœ, about twelve miles northeast of Little Rock. On the next day I ordered Brigadier General Marmaduke, commanding a division of cavalry, to establish his headquarters near Jacksonport, and to dispose his troops so as to observe and retard the movements of the column of Federal cavalry which was then advancing into northeastern Arkansas from Missouri.

Brigadier General Walker, commanding a brigade of cavalry, was, on the same day, ordered to remain with his command in the vicinity of Helena, for the purpose of watching the enemy in that direction and checking his advance from that point. These were the only troops at my disposal for the defence of Little Rock, except a very weak regiment, a small battalion, and a few unattached companies of cavalry, which I kept on the south side of the Arkansas, picketing the country from Little Rock to Napoleon, and thence to the boundary of Louisiana. Brigadier General Steele, commanding in the Indian territory, was already hard pressed by the enemy, and on the defensive, and could not spare a man.

I wrote to the Lieutenant General commanding the department, on the 27th of July, communicating these facts to him, and stating that, whilst I should attempt to defend Little Rock, as the capital of the State and the key to the important valley of the Arkansas, I did not believe it would be possible for me to hold it with the force under my command.

About this time I commenced the construction of a line of rifle pits and other defensive works on the north side of the Arkansas, and about two and a half miles in front of Little Rock, and pushed them forward to completion as rapidly as I could.

The continued advance of Davidson's column of Federal cavalry making it hazardous to retain Walker's brigade any longer on the eastern side of White river, I ordered him, on the 2d of August, to move it to the western side of that stream. As soon as this was done, the enemy unveiled his intention to cross White river at Clarendon, and I consequently moved Walker's brigade, and Marmaduke's division of cavalry, both under command of Brigadier General L. M. Walker, to that vicinity.

Tappan's brigade (which had been detached from my division several months before, and which had been ordered back to Arkansas by Lieutenant General Smith) having reached Little Rock, whither I had ordered it to move by rapid marches, I directed Brigadier General Frost to move his brigade to northern side of the river, and to assume command of my division, which comprised all the infantry near Little Rock, except Tappan's brigade, which I held in reserve on the south side of the river.

Seeing that the position on Bayou Metœ could be easily turned, and that it was otherwise untenable, I ordered General Frost, at the same time, to withdraw his entire command within the line of defences, to which I have before referred, and upon which I continued to labor both night and day.

The enemy continued to advance. Meanwhile my cavalry, under Generals Marsh Walker and Marmaduke, falling back before him, but contesting stubbornly every mile, until I ordered General Walker, on the 23d of August, to take position on Bayou Metœ, with the whole of his and Marmaduke's cavalry, and to hold it as long as possible.

About midday, on the 27th of August, he was attacked in this position, by the enemy, in greatly superior force, and with considerable spirit. The engagement lasted until dark. My troops, which were under the immediate command of Brigadier General Marmaduke, behaved admirably, and the enemy was repulsed, with heavy loss.

General Walker, fearing, from the indications given, that the enemy was about to flank his position, withdrew his troops after dark. The enemy also retired from the field, leaving his dead unburied. Knowing that if I delayed the removal of the public stores from Little Rock until the eve of its evacuation, the greater part of them would be lost, in consequence of the insufficiency of transportation. I had, very soon after assuming command of the district, ordered the chiefs of the several staff departments to send their stores to Arkadelphia as speedily as possible; removing first such as were least likely to be required by the army. These officers were zealously executing this order when intelligence reached me, (on the 20th of August,) that the enemy was occupying Monroe, Louisiana, in force, and thereby not only endangering the valuable stores at Camden, but menacing my line of retreat. A few days later, I received a communication from Brigadier General Cabell, informing me that Brigadier General Steele, commanding the Confederate forces in the Indian Territory, was falling back towards Texas, before a superior force, and that he himself had been driven by the enemy from Fort Smith, and was then retreating in the direction of Caddo Gap. These facts necessitated still greater activity in the removal of the public stores from both Camden and Little Rock; and orders to that effect were consequently given.

I continued, meanwhile, to strengthen the defences on the north side of the river, and to perfect the means of communication between the two banks of the Arkansas, so as to be able to throw my forces readily from the one side to the other, and particularly to secure the safe withdrawal of my army from the northern side of the river, in the event of defeat. My troops were at this time in excellent condition, full of enthusiasm, and eager to meet the enemy; but I had barely eight thousand men, of all arms, whilst the enemy had brought against me nearly, or quite, twenty thousand. My only chance of meeting him successfully lay in the possibility that he would attack me in my entrenchments. I would have given him battle confidently, had he done this. But I had little hope that he would do it, as it was comparatively easy for him to turn my position, by crossing the Arkansas below Little Rock. That river was, at that time, fordable in a great many places; and I could not guard it effectually without weakening my force within the the trenches to a dangerous extent. I communicated these facts, at the time, to the Lieutenant General commanding.

There was, during the last days of August and the first days of September, constant skirmishing between the cavalry advance of the two armies, without any marked change, however, in their relative positions, except that the enemy began to develop more plainly his intention to cross the Arkansas below Little Rock. I therefore ordered General Marsh Walker, on the 31st of August, to move his headquarters to some point on the south side of the river, within twelve or fifteen miles of the city, and to assume command of, and concentrate in that vicinity, (in addition to his own brigade,) all the cavalry which was south of the Arkansas and east of Little Rock. I also gave orders, on the 9th of September, for the construction of a line of defences on that side of the river; and the work was immediately begun.

Early on the morning of the 10th, the enemy appeared in heavy force on the north bank of the river, about eight miles below Little Rock. Colonel A. L. Dobbins (upon whom the command of Walker's division had been devolved, by the unfortunate death of that lamented officer,) immediately concentrated his whole disposable force (about twelve hundred men) to dispute his passage. He was, however, embarrassed not only by the fact that the river was fordable in twelve different places within twelve miles of Little Rock—at one of which the enemy actually made a strong feint of crossing—but by the additional fact that the place at which the enemy did finally force the passage was selected with excellent judgment, it being the upper point of a horse-shoe-like bend, upon the three sides of which he planted five batteries. These, after two hours' heavy cannonading, silenced the guns which Colonel Dobbins had opposed to the enemy's passage, and drove them and the supporting cavalry from the peninsula.

I ordered Tappan's brigade to the relief of Dobbins, as soon as I learned that the enemy was seriously threatening to cross the river, and immediately thereafter ordered General Marmaduke to move his division to the south side, to assume command of all the cavalry, to hold the enemy in check until I could withdraw my infantry and artillery from the north side of the river, and, when this had been accomplished, to cover the retreat—the orders for which were at once given. The infantry began to leave the entrenchments at eleven o'clock in the morning. The city was finally evacuated about five o'clock in the afternoon. The trains had been sent to the rear early in the forenoon.

The cavalry, under command of Brigadier General Marmaduke, constituted the rear guard. It was skilfully handled, and behaved admirably.

My infantry, and most of my artillery, reached Arkadelphia on the 14th of September, without any unusual loss of either men or material, and were encamped in that vicinity.

I disposed my cavalry so as to completely cover my front—General Marmaduke occupying the centre, having his headquarters at Rockport; Colonel Dobbins in command of the right, having his at Tulip, and Colonel Monroe in command of the left, having his at Caddo Gap.

I respectfully refer to the reports of Brigadier General Marmaduke and Colonel A. L. Dobbins, for a detailed statement of the operations of their respective commands. They will be forwarded as soon as they shall have been received.

Lieutenant General Holmes resumed command of the district of Arkansas, at Arkadelphia, on the 25th day of September.

I am, Colonel, very respectfully,
Your obedient servant,
STERLING PRICE,
Major General.

Official:
THOMAS L. SNEAD,
Major and Assistant Adjutant General.

REPORT OF COLONEL DOBBINS.

CAMP BRAGG, Nov. 19th, 1863.

Major THOMAS L. SNEAD, *Assistant Adjutant General:*

MAJOR: In obedience to your request, I have the honor herewith to submit a report of the military operations of my command in front of Little Rock, from the time I assumed command of the division, formerly commanded by Brigadier General Walker, on the 6th day of September, until the 10th of the same month. I must here, however, state that this report will necessarily be general in its terms, omitting details, as I am now, and have been, for the last six weeks, separated from my command, and I have now no access to the papers requisite to make a full report.

On the evening of the 6th of September, by an order from Major General Price, I assumed command of Brigadier General Walker's division, consisting of Dobbins' brigade, Arkansas cavalry, and Carter's brigade, Texas cavalry, to which were also attached Johnson's spy company and Denson's company. At this time, one regiment of Dobbins' brigade was encamped on the north side of the Arkansas river, at Ashley's mill, and the remainder were on the south side of the river, near Buck's ford. Carter's brigade, except about one hundred men, and one section of Pratt's battery, were engaged in picketing from Buck's ford, on the Arkansas river, to Gains' landing, on the Mississippi river. On the morning of the 7th, the enemy advanced on the regiment camped at Ashley's mill, driving the same back to the river. Colonel Newton, then commanding the brigade, was present in command. The regiment lost one killed, three wounded and two captured, including Captain Cowley, adjutant of the brigade. The enemy advanced in greatly superior force, and Colonel Newton crossed the river about eight miles below Little Rock, with that portion of his command, fording the same. This was about ten o'clock in the morning. That night the enemy camped at Ashley's mill and Terry's ferry. From that time, until the evening of the 9th, there was continual skirmishing between my scouts and the enemy, and, also, constant firing across the river, with no loss in my command, and with some damage to the enemy—they reporting to have had three killed at Terry's ferry. On the evening of the 9th, the enemy moved down, in considerable force of cavalry and artillery, to Buck's ford, and built up camp fires within sight of the ford. About ten o'clock that night, Colonel Newton reported to me that the enemy were moving their artillery to Terry's ferry and were throwing out lumber, as if they intended building a bridge at that place. I had previously, as soon as I discovered them at Buck's ford, moved to that point about two hundred bales of cotton, and planted my artillery so as to resist their crossing. I, at the same time, reported to Major General Price, commanding the district of Arkansas, that the enemy were in front of me in heavy force of infantry, cavalry and artillery, reported by a citizen, named Calvin Pemberton, (who had that day seen Generals Steele and Davidson,) to be thirty thousand strong, and that I would be unable to prevent their crossing. My command being very much scattered, and there being twelve fords between Little Rock and Buck's ford, a distance of twelve miles, on the morning of the 10th, about three o'clock, I left my camp near Buck's ford, and rode up the bank of the river to ascertain, if possible, what movement the enemy was making, the reports from scouts having been very unsatisfactory and conflicting. When about four miles above Buck's ford, and about two miles above Terry's ferry, I discovered the enemy digging down the bank, and making preparations to cross the river. This was just at daylight. The river here made a bend in the shape of a horse-shoe, the enemy being about the centre of the bend. I immediately ordered a section of Etter's battery, which had previously been attached to my command, to occupy the point opposite to where the enemy was engaged in cutting down the bank, and to open fire on them, which it did. The enemy immediately opened on Etter's battery, from five batteries placed on the opposite bank, and, from the nature of the bend and the position of the batteries, being planted on each side of the horse-shoe, swept the entire point on which Etter's battery was placed. At the same time, the section of Pratt's battery was also hotly engaged with the enemy at Buck's ford, they having made a demonstration of crossing there. Finding that Etter's battery was unable to prevent the enemy from throwing a bridge across the river, I ordered one piece of Pratt's battery to his assistance. It came up and opened on the enemy, but the fire from the enemy's batteries was so terrific that they were unable to hold their position, and, after being engaged about two hours, were compelled to retire, leaving one piece of Etter's battery, which I had brought off afterwards by the cavalry, being soon after the artillery was removed. The enemy crossed the river, I think, at about ten o'clock in the morning. They crossed, first, one regiment of cavalry, followed immediately by the infantry and cavalry in heavy force. I fell back to Bayou Fourche, a distance of about five miles, fighting all the time. When within about one mile of the bayou, I ordered Colonel Newton, with a portion of the brigade commanded by him, about five hundred men, to go back to the bayou and form on the bank, while I remained and held the enemy in check. This he did. I had, as soon as I found the enemy would cross, ordered all the force from Buck's ford to join me, and had the entire force with me, not exceeding twelve hundred men, at the time the enemy crossed the river When I reached Bayou Fourche, about two o'clock, P. M., Colonel Newton had his command formed, ready to receive the enemy. Then I met Brigadier General Marmaduke, with orders to assume command of all the cavalry, and I immediately turned over the command to him. I sent to Major General Price, from time to time, all the information I could obtain in regard to the movements of the enemy, and kept him constantly informed of all their movements. I lost, in the entire action and skirmishing, about sixty-five men in killed, wounded and missing, including one major (Major S. Coley) killed, and one lieutenant (Bowers) killed; one captain wounded and one captain captured. The loss I give from memory alone, and cannot now say how many privates were killed, and how many wounded.

I have the honor to be,
Yours, with high respect,
ARCH. L. DOBBINS,
Colonel, etc.

Official:
THOMAS L. SNEAD,
Major and A. A. General.

BATTTE OF LOOKOUT MOUNTAIN.

REPORT OF MAJOR GENERAL STEVENSON.

HEADQUARTERS STEVENSON'S DIVISION, }
Near Dalton, January 8, 1864. }

To General SAMUEL COOPER,
    Adjutant and Inspector General, C. S. A.:

GENERAL: Seeing in the Richmond journals that General Bragg has submitted his report of the battle of the 24th and 25th of November to the War Department, I take the liberty of forwarding direct, by Lieutenant Patton, aid-de-camp, my report, with those of my subordinate commanders, of the operations of the troops under my command at and near Lookout mountain, on the 24th November, 1863. Copies of all of the accompanying papers have been forwarded to General Bragg through the headquarters of the army of Tennessee.

I am, General, respectfully, your obedient servant,
                      C. L. STEVENSON,
                          Major General.

HEADQUARTERS STEVENSON'S DIVISION, HARDEE'S CORPS, }
Army of Tennessee, Near Dalton, January 2, 1864. }

Colonel GEORGE W. BRENT,
    Assistant Adjutant General:

COLONEL: I have the honor to submit the following report of the operations of the troops of my command, west of Chattanooga creek, on the 24th November, 1863:

On the 12th of November, I was directed to move my division from the position near the tunnel of East Tennessee and Georgia railroad, which it had occupied since its return from East Tennessee, to the extreme left of our infantry lines, the top of Lookout mountain, reporting to Lieutenant General Hardee. On the 14th of November the positions of the troops of his command were assigned by the Lieutenant General: Walker's division, (commanded by Brigadier General Gist,) to occupy that portion of the line which lay west of the Chattanooga creek to the Chattanooga road, at the base of the mountain; Cheatham's division, (commanded by Brigadier General Jackson,) that known as the "Craven house slope," extending from the left of Walker's line to Smith's trail, on the western side of the mountain, and the defence of the mountain was entrusted to my division and a very small and inadequate force of cavalry. The position assigned to me, the table on the top of the mountain, included the pass at "Johnson's Crook," distant eighteen miles. The numerous passes along the western crest to "Nickajack Pass," a distance of about ten miles, were held by infantry, the remainder by the small force of cavalry. The defensive works on the mountain extended across from east to west, at about two and-a-half miles from the point. To guard this extended line, to protect these numerous passes, and to complete with the dispatch, so frequently urged upon me by the General commanding, the line of defence, the work upon which was prosecuted, agreeably to his orders, day and night, and the necessity of watching, with the utmost vigilance, the movements of the heavy force of the enemy threatening my rear at Stephens' Gap and "Johnson's Crook," demanded and received my constant and undivided attention. By personal inspection and reconnoisance, I familiarized myself with the character of the line entrusted to me, but had neither time nor occasion to make myself acquainted with the dispositions made, by the Lieutenant General commanding, for the defence of the rest of the line, further than such information as I acquired by personal observation in visiting and adjusting the posts of my pickets and signal stations, at and near the point of the mountain from which place, in favorable weather, both armies could be plainly discerned.

On the 23d of November, about one o'clock, P. M., my attention was attracted by heavy firing in the valley below. I immediately proceeded to the point of the mountain, from which I could plainly see all the movements of the enemy. I watched them closely until dark, and then hurried off the following dispatch, by signal, both to Lieutenant General Hardee and direct to General Bragg:

"I observed closely, from the point, the movements of the enemy until dark. An object seemed to be to attract our attention. All the troops in sight were formed from centre to left. Those on their right moved to centre. The troops from 'Raccoon' were in line in full sight. If they intend to attack, my opinion is, it will be upon our left. Both of their bridges are gone."

The movements of the enemy and his demonstrations against our right centre were such that in my own mind, I had not the slightest doubt that his purpose was to attract our attention, induce us to concentrate on our right, thereby weakening our left, and then render the acquisition of Lookout mountain practicable for him.

The manœuvre had the desired effect, for, during the evening, Walker's entire division was removed from its position to the extreme right, and the force west of Chattanooga creek thereby diminished more than one-third. After dark, I was informed by Lieutenant General Hardee that he had been ordered to the extreme right, and I was directed to assume command of the troops west of Chattanooga creek. To fill, as far as possible, the vacancy caused by the removal of Walker's division, Jackson's brigade, of Cheatham's division, was removed from the "Craven house slope," and Cumming's brigade, of my own division, from the top of the mountain—General Cumming, as the senior officer present, being placed in command of the two brigades. I was advised by the Lieutenant General commanding to transfer my headquarters to the Craven house, and subsequently to the camp just vacated by him.

Having thus, without the slightest premonition—not only a large portion of the troops, but even the permanent commander having been removed—been placed in command, at night, at a most critical period, over a wing of the army with whose position and disposition, as I have already stated, I had enjoyed no opportunity of making myself acquainted, I at once used every exertion to gain the necessary information, by sending every officer of my staff, and devoting the whole night myself, to riding over and examining the lines. I found the position, at which General Hardee advised me to establish my headquarters, to be on the eastern side of the Chattanooga creek, some distance beyond the extreme right of my line, and at least two and a half miles from the base of the mountain. The distance, and the fact that the situation was most unfavorable for personal observation, determined me to return to the mountain, which afforded this advantage in the highest degree, and I accordingly addressed you the appended communication [A.] On my way back, I examined the whole line, and, at sunrise, reached the Craven house. I found the troops in position, as assigned by Lieutenant General Hardee. Moore's brigade was bivouacked along the eastern side of the mountain, near the Craven house, ready to move at a moments notice to any point to which it should be ordered. I then provided, as well as the means at my disposal permitted, either for an attack upon Cumming or Jackson.

Immediately upon my arrival on the mountain, I directed the lookouts at the point to keep a close watch, and advise me of any movements the enemy might make.

About ten o'clock, A. M., I received from Brigader General Jackson the communication [B] written him by General Walthall, and soon afterwards was informed, by the men at the point, that there was some picket firing on Lookout creek, I immediately rode to the point to see what was going on. The enemy had, by felling trees, constructed three temporary bridges over the creek, and in a short time, forced a passage.

The troops as they crossed formed to cover the passage of the remainder. I immediately sent a staff officer of General Hardee's, (Major W. D. Pickett,) who happened to be with me, to General Jackson, to inform him of what I had seen, and to direct him at once to place all of his troops in position. He reached General Jackson, I suppose, a little after eleven o'clock, A. M. I caused the picket at Smith's trail to be largely increased, and a strong force to be posted as sharpshooters along the crest of the mountain. The artillery, with trails raised, opened with spirit and effect, and was used until the enemy advanced so close under the cliff that the guns could not be sufficiently depressed for the shots to take effect.

General Walthall's pickets and skirmishers extended from the turnpike bridge of Lookout creek to the railroad bridge, and thence, making nearly a right angle, across the northwest slope of the mountain to a point near Smith's trail. The enemy, as Walthall mentions in his report, had threatened to force a passage of the creek on his right, but their real movement was upon the left. A large force had moved up the creek, under cover of the fog, crossed above, and passing along the western slope, attacked him successfully in flank and rear.

Their advance on the flank and from the front, was gallantly contested, but though their front line sometimes wavered, they pressed on, Walthall falling back to the line which I have before mentioned, but with very heavy loss in prisoners, owing to the enemy's taking him in flank and rear.

Finding that the fog was becoming so dense that the troops on the northern point of the mountain could not see the enemy moving upon Walthall, I gave orders for Pettus, with my only disposable force, to move down and report to Brigadier General Jackson. He started at half-past twelve o'clock, and reached the scene of action a little past one o'clock, relieving Walthall on the left of Moore's line. This position was held by Moore, Walthall and Pettus, until about eight o'clock, P. M., when Walthall's and part of Pettus' command were relieved by Clayton's brigade, commanded by Colonel Holtzclaw, which was sent to cover the movement to the right. Moore and Holtzclaw retired from the position about two o'clock, A. M., on the 25th. Brown, finding that the enemy could not be seen for the fog, deployed his sharpshooters down the sides of the mountain, who were guided in firing by the reports of the enemy's musketry; at the same time the men stationed along the creek rolled down rocks in the direction of the Craven house. This, with the shells from the Napoleon guns, doubtless contributed not a little to checking the advance of the enemy, for soon thereafter his firing materially abated. Early in the day, the appended communication [C] was received from General Bragg. A perusal of it will show how highly important he, on that day, considered my making such dispositions as would effectually prevent a severance of the troops which I commanded from the main body of the army. About the time the attack was made on Walthall, the enemy massed a considerable force upon the Chattanooga road, in front of Cumming's line, evidently for the purpose of co-operating with, and making a diversion in favor of, their assaulting column. The number of his troops massed for this purpose, who had been in plain sight until the view was obscured by the mist, the serious weakness of Cumming's force, there not being a man for yards upon some parts of the line, and the certainty, that to reinforce the command near the Craven house from Cumming, was to give the enemy an opportunity to cut us off from the main body, without even a show of resistance, rendered it highly improper to withdraw a man from him. I have already stated that he had but two brigades to hold the line from the Chattanooga creek to the Chattanooga road, at the base of the mountain. The force, early that morning at the Craven house slope, had consisted of two brigades—Moore's and Walthall's—and was now reinforced by the larger part of a third, (Pettus',) while in the mountain top there was but one small brigade and two regiments of another, the larger portion being between the point and the works, the other picketing and holding a line of about ten miles.

Of my six brigades, it will be perceived, from the foregoing accounts, that four were engaged, while the remaining two were threatened by a force which, had it advanced, could soon have driven them from their position and immediately cut us off from the army east of the creek, a position which I had been instructed to hold, even at the expense of the mountain. I had been directed by General Bragg, if I needed reinforcements, to call for them, [see letter C,] and as soon as I saw that the enemy were attacking and would carry the point, I availed myself of the order, and called both upon Generals Breckinridge and Bragg for them, by a staff officer. I instructed him to say to them that, if they would send me reinforcements, I would, when the fog rose, attack the enemy in flank by sharpshooters in the mountain crest, and, descending Smith's trail, take him in rear, and, I doubted not, drive him from the slope. This statement I repeated by three other staff officers, sent at intervals of half an hour. After waiting for some time for an answer, I received a verbal order from General Bragg to the effect that no reinforcements could be sent me; that I must withdraw as best I could under cover of the fog, and that a brigade would be sent to the base of the mountain to cover the withdrawal. Subsequently I received the following note:

"TWO AND A HALF O'CLOCK, P. M.

"The General commanding, instructs me to say that you will withdraw your command from the mountain to this side of Chattanooga creek, destroying the bridges behind. Fight the enemy as you retire. The thickness of the fog will enable you to retire, it is hoped, without much difficulty."

About five hours after the date of this order, I received a note from Major General Breckinridge, then my corps commander, informing me that he had arrived at the base of the mountain, with a brigade, (Clayton's,) to be used in the retirement, and generously offering to confer with me, and render me any assistance in his power in the withdrawal of the troops. This brigade, as has been heretofore stated, relieved Walthall's and part of Pettus' command, about eight o'clock, P. M., and was the only force sent to me on that day. I was engaged in issuing the necessary orders for the retirement of the troops when Major General Cheatham arrived. He informed me that he had come to consult with me, but not to assume command.

I sent the troops from the top of the mountain down, and then proceeded myself to a point near its base, where General Cheatham and myself had appointed to meet. Here, as senior officer, he assumed command, and I then gave no further directions with regard to the retirement of the troops, except such as I received from him for those of my own division. Here we met also Major General Breckinridge, who, when Major General Cheatham took command, returned to his corps. Brown was directed at once to cross Chattanooga creek—about eleven o'clock, P. M.—commencing at one o'clock; and Cheatham's division, with which was (then) serving Pettus' brigade, of my own division afterwards—all with directions to await further orders on the eastern side. General Cheatham then left me, as I understood, to get further orders from General Bragg. Except for about one hour—from about half-past ten to half-past eleven, A M.—the mountain was enveloped in fog during the day.

About twelve o'clock, M., two staff officers of General Bragg rode up to where I was, (General Cumming's quarters,) and, stating that they could not find General Cheatham, handed me orders to him from General Bragg, to send all the troops that had been west of Chattanooga creek to the extreme right. This order was immediately given, and was executed as quickly as possible. The conduct of the troops was all that could have been desired, and they accomplished all that could have been expected of them.

The withdrawal of Walker's division, on the night of the 23d, in my opinion, rendered the position on the left—opposed by so large a force—untenable, and it was beyond the power of the troops then to do more than secure the communication with the top of the mountain, and with the main body of the army, until General Bragg could decide whether he would reinforce them sufficiently to hold the line or abandon it. This decision I have already given. The mountain was held until two o'clock the next morning, and the troops, artillery and trains were withdrawn in order to the eastern side of the creek.

As Brigadier General Jackson is mentioned, in the reports of subordinate commanders, as having been absent from his headquarters with me, it is due to him to state that, having checked the enemy in rear of the Craven house, and finding that they had massed a considerable force on the Chattanooga road, apparently with the intention of advancing from that direction—it being important that he should have definite orders in case they should make a successful attack upon the troops on that part of the line, and thus cut us off from the main body of the army—to provide against any accident in transmission of such orders, he came to me to receive them in person. I approved of his course, under the circumstances. As his conduct, at the battle of Missionary Ridge, when not under my command, has been alluded to in one of the accompanying reports, I append, at his request, to be read with said report, a communication [D] addressed him on the subject by his commanding officer, Major General Cheatham.

I take pleasure in expressing my indebtedness to Major W. D. Pickett, of Lieutenant General Hardee's staff, and my renewed obligations to Majors John J. Reeve, George L. Gillespie, J. H. F. Mayo, H. M.

Matthews, H. Webb, J. E. McElrath, and Chief Surgeon H. M. Compton, of my staff.

For the particular service rendered by the several regiments, I respectfully ask attention to the reports of brigade commanders. I transmit herewith maps of the lines west of Chattanooga creek.

Delay in the reports of subordinate commanders, and my illness, have prevented me from forwarding this report sooner.

I have the honor to be, very respectfully,
Your obedient servant,
C. L. STEVENSON,
Major General.

[A.]

HEADQUARTERS FORCES WEST OF CHATTANOOGA CREEK,
Hardee's Headquarters, November 24, 1863.

To Colonel G. W. BRENT,
Assistant Adjutant General, Army of Tennessee:

COLONEL: Agreeably to a suggestion in a letter from Lieutenant Colonel Roy, General Hardee's assistant adjutant general, I came to this place to-night to establish my headquarters, but I find that I am on the opposite side of the creek, and some distance from the extreme right of my line.

I will return quickly to the mountain, which is more central, from which I can overlook my whole command, communicate, by signal, from my entreme left to right, and by couriers, in case of fog, from stations which I have established at the base of the mountain.

I am, Colonel, respectfully, your obedient servant,
C. L. STEVENSON,
Major General commanding.

[B.]

HEADQUARTERS WALTHALL'S BRIGADE,
Craven House, Nov. 24, 1863, 8 o'clock, A. M.

MAJOR: It is foggy this morning, and nothing can be distinctly seen, but I feel sure the enemy's pontoons have both disappeared, and most of the tents in Chattanooga have been removed. Troops are moving rapidly to the left, in what numbers it is difficult to estimate. The lines of the enemy, in front of their works, visible on yesterday, are still to be seen. They seem to have bivouacked there. A steamboat is busy in the river beyond the town from here.

The fog has thickened so within the last thirty minutes that I can see nothing.
Very respectfully, your obedient servant,
E. C. WALTHALL,
Brigadier General.

Respectfully forwarded to Major General Stevenson. The original has been sent direct to army headquarters.
JOHN K. JACKSON,
Brigadier General commanding Cheatham's Division.

A true copy:
C. L. STEVENSON,
Major General.

[C.]

HEADQUARTERS ARMY OF TENNESSEE,
Missionary Ridge, November 24, 1863.

Major General STEVENSON,
Commanding Division:

GENERAL: The General commanding directs me to say that you are charged with the defence, on the left of Chattanooga creek. If the enemy attempt to cross the creek you must defend obstinately, calling on the forces to your left and also on Breckinridge on your right for assistance. Should you be compelled to yield, the force on the mountain and at "Craven house" must be withdrawn in time to save them from being cut off. In a last resort, the "Craven house" command could pass on the old road leading up the mountain, and form a junction with the force coming down; or, in case of extreme necessity, they could move south on the mountain, but this is only an extreme case.

Report fully and frequently by letter and signal all the movements in our front.
I am, General, very respectfully,
K. FALCONER,
Assistant Adjutant General.

A true copy:
C. L. STEVENSON,
Major General.

HEADQUARTERS CHEATHAM'S DIVISION,
January 3, 1864.

General JOHN K. JACKSON:

SIR: Your note of 31st December is before me. In it you say: "As my (your) report of the battle of Lookout mountain will not pass through you, I will be greatly obliged to you for your opinion of my conduct on Missionary Ridge, on 25th November last, with liberty to use it officially or otherwise, as I may see proper."

In reply, I have to say that I saw nothing wrong in your conduct on Missionary Ridge, on the 25th November last. You were always present to receive and obey my orders, as far as could be done, amidst the confusion of the day. I left yourself and General Walthall with orders to hold the position then occupied for thirty minutes, and then to follow on to Chickamauga. All of which was promptly complied with.

Yours, very respectfully,
B. F. CHEATHAM,
Major General, C. S. A.

A true copy:
C. L. STEVENSON,
Major General.

REPORT OF BRIGADIER GENERAL WALTHALL.

ATLANTA, Ga., Dec. 13, 1863.

Major JAMES D. PORTER,
A. A. A. G., Cheatham's Division:

MAJOR: I have the honor to submit the following report of the part taken by my command in the affair on Lookout mountain, on 24th November, 1863:

About dark, on the evening of the 23rd, I received orders from the Brigadier General commanding to hold my command in readiness to move at a day's notice, and later in the night, to have three days' rations prepared; but, in view of the movements of the enemy on the previous day, my command, which occupied a position on the west side of Lookout mountain and near the northern slope, was ordered to stand "to arms" before daylight on the 24th November. My picket line which extended along Lookout creek from the turnpike bridge near its mouth, to the railroad bridge across it, and thence up the mountain side to the cliff, was strengthened by increasing its reserves early in the morning, troops having been observed moving rapidly up the creek. The fog at that time being very dense, it was impossible to estimate the number of the troops in motion, and this fact (as well as what seemed to be the state of things in Chattanooga and on the river,) was reported to the Brigadier General commanding. Shortly thereafter, the fog having been partially dissipated in the valley, (though it still obscured the crest of the mountain above,) with Brigadier General Moore, the ranking officer at hand, I observed the movements of the enemy across Lookout creek, from a point near the right of my command, and saw a brigade take position in front of that part of my picket line between the two bridges, of which one regiment was thrown forward, and soon the pickets were engaged. Brigadier General Moore returned to his command, it being agreed between us that he would notify the Brigadier General commanding of what had been observed. Rude breastworks of logs and stones had been constructed on the mountain side by the command which had occupied the ground before me, running parellel to the mountain and the creek, and along these my command, except the thirty-fourth Mississippi regiment, with which the picket reserves had been strengthened, was formed, awaiting the development of th eneemy's purpose; it being uncertain whether he would pass across the creek on the right, as the movements discovered would seem to indicate, or would approach from the left of the picket line with the troops which had already moved in that direction

Soon after the firing commenced across the creek, two batteries which had previously been erected on the ridge beyond Lookout creek, (of which, in conversation with the Brigadier General commanding, I had more than once made mention,) opened upon my main line, less than three-quarters of a mile distant; and while these batteries were shelling, two pieces of artillery were planted at a point between the creek and the river, which, though across the creek from my picket line, was yet, by reason of the course of the stream, in rear of much of that part of the line which took the direction of the creek. Major Johnson, commanding thirtieth, and Colonel Brantley, commanding twenty-ninth Mississippi regiments, occupying positions nearest to it, had been instructed to support that part of the picket line which extended up the mountain side from the railroad and bridge, should the enemy approach from that direction; and the other regiments, twenty-seventh Mississippi, under Lieutenant Colonel Jones, and twenty-fourth Mississippi, under Colonel Dowd, were held ready to move to the right or left as occasion might require.

While writing a communication to inform the Brigadier General commanding of the position of the pieces in the angle of the creek, (with the suggestion that a single piece in a position which had been prepared for artillery, could silence them, and that this done, I thought I could hold the force in check,) I received information, through scouts sent out up the creek, to observe the movements of the enemy; that a force had crossed the creek above the angle in the picket line. I added this to the communication and sent it to the Brigadier General commanding by one of his staff officers. In the meantime, Brigadier General Moore had applied to me to know the position of my line, as he was ordered to form on my right, and I learned from a staff officer of the Brigadier General commanding that such would be General Moore's position. I informed both where my line then was, and Captain Moreno, of the staff of the Brigadier General commanding, went with me, at my request, and looked at my position, but that the direction which would ultimately be given my line would necessarily depend upon the direction from which the enemy, then engaging my pickets on the right and threatening my left, almost at right angles to the part engaged, might make his main attack. Meanwhile the firing from the batteries beyond the creek, which before had been irregular, became constant and heavy, and soon the enemy advanced on the left, in three lines running across the mountain side. Such resistance as I could offer a force like this, (consisting, as the Federal General Thomas, in an official dispatch to his Government, says, of Geary's division and two brigades of another corps,) was made with my small command, nearly one-third of which was covering a picket line more than a mile in extent. While the twenty-ninth and thirtieth Missisippi regiments, in support of the picket line, were resisting the enemy in the position assigned them, (to cover which, it had been necessary to take intervals,) and when the immense numbers of the enemy had been discovered, the twenty-seventh and part of the twenty-fourth Mississippi regiments were put in position several hundred yards in rear of the picket line, where, being sheltered from the enemy's small arms, and reserving their fire till the regiments and pickets in front had passed behind them in falling back, they delivered a destructive fire upon the advancing lines. The front line wavered and then was broken at one point, but after falling back a short distance, it soon reformed, and, despite my rapid and well-directed fire, moved steadily and irresistibly forward, pressing heaviest upon my extreme left. I endeavored, in falling back, to turn the rocks and irregularities of the ground to the best account for the protection of the men, and retiring from one position of strength to another, to yield the ground as slowly as possible, with the hope that support (for which I had sent to General Moore) might reach me. Many officers and men were captured because they held their positions so long as to render escape impossible, the ground in their rear being rocky, rugged, and covered with fallen timber. My command being greatly sheltered, were enabled to inflict upon the enemy, as he advanced, a loss far greater than it sustained.

By twelve o'clock, M., or about that time, and two and a half or three hours after the first picket firing began, I was driven to the ridge which runs down the northern slope of the mountain, where, with three companies of sharpshooters from the twenty-fourth Mississippi regiment, which had previously been posted there, (and afterwards strengthened by another from the same regiment,) I made an effort to retard the enemy's progress, till the remainder of my command, including the pickets on the right, then in charge of Colonel J. A. Campbell, twenty-seventh Mississippi regiment, could pass across the northern slope of the mountain. The slope was commanded by the casemated batteries on Moccasin point, from which my command was constantly shelled, from the time the slope was reached till they had passed across it. This passage was effected, in part, by means of a rifle pit, designed for the double purpose of a covered way and defence against an attack from a northern direction, which runs across that part of the slope west of Craven's house; the sharpshooters on the ridge, meanwhile, resisting the enemy's advance as far as they were able, being themselves subjected to a heavy fire from the Moccasin guns. After passing Craven's house, between half past twelve and one o'clock, P. M., or about that time, I dispatched a staff officer to the Brigadier General commanding, to advise him of my movements. Most of my picket line, to the right of the railroad bridge, (which had been forced back upon the reserves, in the rifle pits at the foot of the mountain, and then were unable to check the force opposing them,) were cut off, including the efficient officer in charge of it, an ineffectual effort having been made, as soon as the enemy began to overwhelm me on the left, to retire it up the steep mountain side, before the advancing lines, sweeping along the west side of the mountain, could occupy the slope near Craven's house. The only pathway leading from the right of the position held by the picket line to Craven's house, ran up the creek to a point near the railroad bridge, and then obliquely (in its general direction) across the side of the mountain to the northern slope, forming an acute angle near the bridge. When the left was forced back, this angle was possessed by the enemy, and then the picket force on the right had to be withdrawn up a rugged steep, broken and rocky, and difficult of passage even for a footman at leisure. The character of the ground making it impossible to communicate through mounted men with different parts of the line; the overwhelming force of the enemy; the advantageous posi-

tions of his batteries beyond the creek; the extent and direction of my picket line, and the fact that my only outlet, when forced to retire, was across a point commanded by the Moccasin guns, all operated to produce confusion in the withdrawal of my command to a point on the east side of the mountain, without the direct range of these guns. The point selected was about four hundred yards from Craven's house, where my line extended from the road up to the cliff.
About one o'clock, P. M., I checked the enemy's advance, which was heaviest on my left, and was soon informed that reinforcements would be sent me, by a staff officer of the Brigadier General commanding. In the course of half an hour, or three quarters of an hour, Brigadier General Pettus came up, with his command, in fine order, and moved promptly upon the line I occupied, engaging the enemy at once, and with spirit, and enabling me to withdraw my command and replenish my ammunition (then well-nigh exhausted) from my ordnance train, which I had ordered up to the road in my rear. This done, I formed my command, under cover, immediately in his rear, for his support at such point as it might be needed. Soon afterwards, through one of his staff officers, he requested me to send him support on his left, and I immediately ordered Colonel Brantley, twenty-ninth Mississippi regiment, with his own regiment, the thirtieth Mississippi, and a small detachment of the thirty-fourth, to support this part of his line, and in a few moments the remainder of my command was moved up, to strengthen the line, which, along its whole length, was hotly engaged. I directed Colonel Brantly to advance his left, as far as it could be done, without leaving an interval between his line and the cliff, so as to get the benefit of an oblique fire upon the line which was passing before us. This order was executed with that officer's characteristic promptness.

In the meantime orders were received from Major General Stevenson, through Major Ingram of the staff of the Brigadier General commanding, to hold the line then occupied till reinforcements should arrive, when an advance would be made, and the force on the mountain would co-operate; and from the Brigadier General commanding, through a staff officer, that the position would be held as long as possible, and, if forced to retire, that I would fall back up the mountain. Later in the evening an order reached me from the latter to hold my position, if possible, till ordered to retire. General Pettus' command, and my own, held the position all the afternoon, (during the most of which time it was so hazy and misty that objects could not be well distinguished, except at a short distance,) and until long after nightfall, when, having been relieved by Colonel Holtzclaw with his brigade, I withdrew my command to the road leading down the mountain in the rear, and then remained till about eleven o'clock, when, under orders from Major General Cheatham, I moved my command to McFarland's spring, where it passed the remainder of the night.

At no time, during this prolonged struggle, whose object was to prevent the occupation of the enemy first, of the important point near Craven's house, and afterwards the only road from the mountain, leading from Major General Stevenson's position to the main body of the army, did I have the benefit of my division commander's personal presence. Reference has been made to such orders as reached me from him. After I was relieved, and while awaiting orders to move, I saw him for the first time, on his way, as he told me, to see the General-in-chief.

The casualties of my command cannot be correctly reported, inasmuch as the killed and many of the wounded fell into the enemy's hands. The accompanying list, to which I respectfully refer, only shows among the killed and wounded such as are were known certainly to be so, and cannot, for want of positive information, embrace a large number, particularly of the pickets and their reserves on the right, who are supposed to have fallen, as they were long subjected to a very heavy fire both from artillery and small arms, but of whose loss, further than that they fell into the enemy's hands, no report can be had.

I regret that, for want of a competent person to prepare one, I am unable to submit herewith an accurate map of the ground I occupied, and its surroundings, as it would contribute greatly to a perfect understanding of movements and events as related.

No copies of the dispatches forwarded during the morning, having been retained, and as I am unable to obtain such now, I have been compelled to give them from memory.

The officers and men of my command, with a few exceptions, did their duty well in this engagement; but it is due in particular to commend Colonel W. F. Brantley, twenty-ninth Mississippi regiment, and Lieutenant Colonel R. P. MacIlvaine, twenty-fourth Mississippi regiment, for the skill, activity, zeal and courage I have ever observed in them under similar circumstances, but which, in an especial degree, signalized their action on this occasion.

The latter officer was not with his regiment during the engagement west of the mountain, having been previously assigned to duty on the picket line, where he rendered me important aid. Major John Ingram, assistant adjutant general to the Brigadier General commanding, was with me during most of the afternoon, and I am pleased here to signify my high appreciation of his gallantry, and the valuable assistance I received at his hands, in his bearing my orders and otherwise.

To Lieutenants John C. Harrison, A. A. A. G., and George M. Govan, assistant inspector general, of my own staff, I am indebted for the promptness, gallantry and efficiency with which all their duties upon the field were discharged.

I submit herewith the reports of the regimental commanders, showing many details, not incorporated herein.

Respectfully, your obedient servant,
E. C. WALTHALL,
Brigadier General

REPORT OF BRIGADIER GENERAL CUMMING.

HEADQUARTERS CUMMING'S BRIGADE,
Near Dalton, Dec. 5, 1863.

Major JOHN J. REEVE,
    Assistant Adjutant General :,

MAJOR : I have the honor to submit the following report of the operations of my brigade on the 24th and 25th of November :

About four o'clock, on the afternoon of the 23rd ultimo, I received an order from Major General Stevenson, commanding forces on the left, to form my brigade as quickly as possible, to vacate the position which I had occupied for the previous eight or ten days, on the mountain, and to proceed to occupy the line which had just been vacated by General Gist's (Walker's) division. I was, at the same time, informed that Jackson's brigade, commanded by Colonel Wilkerson, would assist me in holding the line in question, and that he had already been directed to report to me. Owing to the darkness and the exceeding badness of the road, and the number of wagons met going up the mountain, the brigade did not reach the line until about nine o'clock, P. M. I found Colonel Wilkerson already in the trenches, and placed my brigade on his right. When thus placed in position the two brigades rested with the right on Chattanooga creek and the left on the road to Chattanooga, which passes by the foot of Lookout mountain.

In consequence of the great length of the line (upwards of a mile) when compared with the smallness of the force on hand for its defence, I considered the position to be exceedingly weak. Fortunately, however, neither on that night nor during the next day, did the enemy manifest any disposition to attack us. The next day we witnessed, without being able to render them any assistance, the disaster which befell our troops on the mountain.

About ten o'clock, on the night of the 24th instant, Major General Cheatham, who had, in the course of the day, arrived upon the ground, and, by virtue of seniority, superseded Major General Stevenson in command, visited my headquarters, at the Gillespie house, in company with Major General Stevenson and Brigadier General Jackson. The order of detail was at that time given by Major General Cheatham for the withdrawal of the troops from the west side of Chattanooga creek. By the term of this order, my command (two brigades) withdrew last, and at an hour arranged with reference to the withdrawal of the other brigades from the mountain, half-past two o'clock being designated as the hour for my brigade to retire, and three o'clock for my picket to be recalled. The order of Major General Cheatham also directed that the troops having withdrawn should be established in line of battle on the east side of the creek.

Shortly after this, Major General Cheatham withdrew, leaving Major General Stevenson in command at that point. A short time before the arrival of the hour designated for the withdrawal of my command, a staff officer of the General commanding reached the quarters with directions that all the troops should be withdrawn as rapidly as possible from that side of the creek, and that instead of forming line of battle after having crossed, they should be marched with all possible dispatch to the right, and report to Lieutenant General Hardee. It being within a few minutes of the time designated for the withdrawal of my brigade by Major General Cheatham, and the road being now occupied by the troops which preceded mine, Major General Stevenson deemed it not advisable to change the time indicated in the order of Major General Cheatham.

At half-past two o'clock, I withdrew, and having reached the Gillespie house, directed Wilkerson's brigade to cross the creek by the upper bridge, and report there to Brigadier General Jackson. My own brigade crossed at the lower bridge, passed through the valley and ascended the ridge by the road on the right of General Bragg's headquarters. After reaching the top of the ridge we were subjected to a fire of shell. At this time, I dispatched a staff officer to find the headquarters of Lieutenant General Hardee and report my arrival.

During his absence, I was met by the General commanding and directed by him to push on with all possible speed to the right. Soon afterwards, Maj. General Stevenson, who had been in conference with the commanding General, directed me to halt my brigade until his division took up its position in line of battle on Missionary ridge about half-past nine o'clock. In this line my brigade, which was the centre of the division, had its right resting upon the top of the tunnel. In front of the position occupied by the right two regiments, a wide gorge, of not very steep descent but considerable grown up with the thicket, descended into the plain beneath, and at the foot of which were a collection of houses about two hundred yards from the line. Beyond these houses the country spread out in open fields in all directions. Upon my right, and somewhat in my front, was a strong position on a knob partially fortified and held by a portion of Major General Cleburne's troops, and upon which it soon became evident the enemy proposed to make a powerful assault.

Shortly after taking position in line of battle, the skirmishers of the enemy appeared in the open country behind the houses (a long line) advancing upon our line, and supported by heavy columns in the rear. Seeing them advancing upon the houses heretofore mentioned, Lieutenant General Hardee had directed me to send down two regiments to take possession of the houses and hold them, but if compelled to retire to burn them. The thirty-ninth Georgia regiment, Colonel J. T. McConnell commanding, and the fifty-sixth Georgia regiment, Lieutenant Colonel J. I. Slaughter commanding, (the right two regiments,) were designed as the ones to perform this movement. They passed down the ridge, one on the right and the other on the left of the railroad, and engaged the enemy's skirmishers to the rear and right of the houses. Here a brisk skirmish fight occurred between the two regiments and a brigade of the enemy, but at long distance, and resulting in little loss on either side. A considerable amount of ammunition having been wasted, and the two regiments being apparently threatened by a movement of the enemy on their right flank, who had advanced in heavy columns towards the battery on the fortified knob on our right, orders were given them by Major General Stevenson to retake their position on the ridge. This movement was effected in perfect order, under a dropping fire from the enemy's sharpshooters. Owing to some misconception of orders, the troops withdrew without setting fire to the houses.

During the absence of the right two regiments, the left two regiments, the thirty-sixth Georgia, Lieutenant Colonel Wallace, and the thirty-fourth Georgia, Colonel Johnson, were moved up to supply their position in the line, and the returned regiments formed in their rear while replenishing their cartridge boxes. While the left two were being brought to supply the place of the right two regiments, each of them sustained a serious loss in the wounding of its commanding officer. Colonel J. A. W. Johnson, thirty-fourth Georgia, being struck by a minie ball in the leg, and Lieutenant Colonel Wallace, thirty-sixth Georgia, having received a severe contusion from the fragment of a shell. In the placing *hors de combat* of these two brave and experienced officers upon the eve of a hot encounter, I felt that the brigade, as well as their respective regiments, had sustained a serious loss.

His regiment having been supplied with ammunition, the gallant Colonel McConnell requested to be allowed to take it again to the foot of the hill and drive the enemy from the houses and vicinity. This permission was not accorded, but subsequently he was directed to send four companies to set fire to the houses. This was successfully performed by Captain Milton, who took possession of the houses, burnt them and rejoined his regiment, bringing off with him nine prisoners, and sustaining but little loss.

Shortly after this operation, about one o'clock, P. M., I received an order from Major General Stevenson to send one regiment of my brigade to report to Major General Cleburne to continue the left of his line from the direction of the knob, hitherto mentioned towards the railroad. This duty was assigned to the thirty-ninth Georgia, which, forming in line of battle, marched to the position indicated. Immediately afterwards, I received directions to send another regiment to the same point and with the same instructions. The thirty-fourth Georgia, commanded now by Lieutenant Colonel Bradley, was sent. The two regiments last referred to, in the position they now occupied, held the crest of the ridge between the fortified point, heretofore referred to, and the railroad. Immediately upon their arrival at their respective positions, each regiment, in succession, became hotly engaged with the enemy, who occupied a declivity behind a ridge about thirty yards from the ridge occupied by our troops. At this point the gallant Colonel McConnell fell, shot through the head with a rifle ball. Actuated by a zealous desire to place his troops in a position where they could be most effectively employed against the enemy, he rode forward to the front and right of his regiment. In this he was plainly exposed to the view of the enemy's line. His life fell a sacrifice to his zeal and fidelity to the public cause. In his death the Confederacy lost a most gallant and meritorious soldier, and the State of Georgia a most useful and patriotic citizen.

While the two regiments last referred to had been taking up their position on Cleburne's left, the other two regiments of the brigade, the fifty-sixth and thirty-sixth Georgia, had been conducted by the Brigadier General, in person, in rear of the fortified knob. Shortly after attaining this position, an order was received from Major General Stevenson to send another regiment to Cleburne's left. The fifty-sixth Georgia was formed and marched in line of battle up the knoll, the brigade commander directing its movements in person. Before attaining the crest of the ridge, I encountered Major General Cleburne, to whom I reported, and by whom I was directed to carry the regiment to the highest point of the knob, and to the nearest place behind the breastworks where it would be sheltered, and to retain that position. In attaining this position the regiment was subjected to a very heavy fire, during which Lieut. Colonel Slaughter fell, wounded in the leg by a fragment of shell.

Upon my appearance on the hill, I was met by several officers of the rank of colonel, whose troops were engaged in the breastworks, and who were acquainted with the situation of affairs, who advised me that our troops in the outer line were being shot down by the enemy, who was completely under shelter, and that a brisk, effective charge at that point would probably succeed in driving him from the front of the works. I was advised, at the same time, of an opening of forty or fifty yards in the breastworks, immediately in my front, through which I could make the charge. I at once approved the idea, but felt that another regiment would be necessary to its successful prosecution, and 1 desired, likewise, to obtain the consent of the Major General commanding to the measure. I at once dispatched my assistant adjutant general, Captain Phinizy, to bring on the thirty-sixth Georgia regiment. At the same time a messenger was sent to Major General Cleburne to ask his assent to the proposed charge. The thirty-sixth Georgia was very shortly brought up and placed in rear of the fifty-sixth, and about ten paces from it. These regiments were commanded at this time respectively by Captain Grice and Captain Morgan. Calling these officers, together with several other of the senior officers of the regiments around me, I explained to them, in detail, the movement about to be executed, and the mode of proceeding that I desired them to adopt. This was, substantially, to push forward, on the word being given, at the "double-quick," passing over every obstacle that they might encounter, breaking over the breastworks and the men that line them, when they should reach that point, and engage the enemy with the bayonet, not opening fire until he should commence to give way.

I observed, upon the part of the commanders just mentioned, as well as their subordinates, a manifest disposition to perform the work required at their hands with zeal and alacrity. The rank and file of the regiments also seemed to be moved by a desire to engage the enemy in a hand to hand conflict.

The charge was not delayed by Major General Cleburne. We

had but completed all preparations for it, when an order was brought me from that officer to move forward on the charge and engage the enemy. Immediately the word was given, the men stood up in their ranks, and at the word "forward," rushed on, with a cheer; one regiment following immediately in rear of the other. On arriving at the open space, heretofore mentioned as existing between the two positions of our breastworks on the hill, it was found that this opening was only sufficiently extensive to admit the passage out of one-third of the regimental front. This compelled the men upon the flank of the regiments to make their way out by climbing over the men in the ditches and the breastworks. This unavoidably created some confusion, which was added to by a heavy volley poured in by the enemy.

By the energetic exertion of the officers, the two regiments were, however, in a few moments reformed and started forward. The two regiments of the brigade upon our left, who, up to this time, had not been acting in conjunction with us, being apprised of the charge being made by their comrades on the right, under the direction of their regimental commanders, moved forward and engaged the enemy in their front, thus supporting us on the left, and making the charge—one of brigade front—all along the line. The charge was entirely successful. The men, exhibiting great bravery and determination, and, gallantly led on by their officers, met the enemy in a short but decisive hand-to-hand encounter, and drove him over the slope on which he had been posted. The enemy which was immediately in front of us took shelter behind rocks and trees, and, supported by heavy columns in his rear, kept up a brisk and galling fire upon us. This fire was returned with spirit by our troops, who, however, having been considerably broken up by the nature of the ground traversed, and by the sharp conflict with the enemy, gradually drew back to the top of the ridge, in the neighborhood of the rifle-pits, the enemy closing up behind us cautiously and slowly, without any disposition to charge.

Having readjusted the line, and given the command for ten or fifteen minutes' rest, the charge was again called, and the troops a third time rushed down the hill-side with great courage and alacrity, and, charging upon the enemy in the flat, in a short time completely routed him and drove him in confusion beyond his supports. The troops retained their positions at the foot of the slope until their dead and wounded were brought in. There being no further indication of an advance upon the part of the enemy, the brigade was then drawn behind the breastworks, and rested on its arms, in rear of certain fresh troops who were found in that position.

Shortly after our withdrawal to the point designated, I received an order from Major General Cleburne to move my brigade down the ridge towards the left. After moving about half a mile to the left, I found the head of my column approaching a line of battle, drawn up at right angles to the ridge. On riding forward, I ascertained it was Brigadier General Brown's brigade. On consultation with that officer, I was advised to retain my (then) position until instructions should be received from Lieutenant General Hardee. At this moment the enemy opened fire upon the troops that were in front of Brigadier General Brown, and, those troops giving back, General Brown's brigade was faced about and marched to the rear, pursuant to orders previously given him. This produced some little confusion in my troops, which was, however, shortly rectified, and they were marched forward and placed in line of battle on General Brown's right, and in continuation of his line. Immediately thereafter we received orders from Major General Cheatham to move our troops from the field by the left flank, moving towards Chickamauga Depot. This was effected under cover of night, and without loss or confusion.

In a contest in which all concerned bore themselves so well, it is impossible to particularize. The regiments all conducted themselves with distinguished gallantry. In the several charges, five colors and many prisoners were taken by the brigade. The commanders of the fifty-sixth and thirty-eighth Georgia regiments (Captains Grice and Morgan) managed their regiments with great boldness and energy. The brigade commander also received valuable assistance from Acting Adjutant Brewster, of the fifty-sixth regiment.

Captains Cody, Wise and Phinizy, and Lieutenant Steiner, of my staff, were with me during the engagement, and were especially active and prompt in discharge of their duty. They rendered valuable aid in encouraging and leading on the troops. In the final charge, Captain Cody, acting assistant inspector general, had his leg broken by a musket ball, and Lieutenant Steiner, my aid-de-camp, was wounded in the hand by a fragment of shell.

I send herewith a list of casualties.

I am, Major, respectfully, your obedient servant,

A. CUMMING,
Brigadier General.

REPORT OF BRIGADIER GENERAL BROWN.

HEADQUARTERS BROWN'S BRIGADE,
November 30, 1863.

To Major J. J. REEVE,
Assistant Adjutant General, Stevenson's Division:

MAJOR: I beg to submit a report of the part performed by my command in the battle of Lookout mountain and Missionary ridge, the 20th and 25th of November, 1863.

On Monday night, 23d of November, Major General Stevenson directed me to take command of his division, then occupying the summit of Lookout mountain and defending the approaches at that point and on the west slope of the mountain as far as Nichojack trail, a distance of ten miles. At twelve o'clock that night, I was ordered by the Major General to send Cumming's brigade to the base of Lookout mountain to report to Brigadier General Jackson, and Haggerty's battery of Parrott guns to report to Brigadier General Anderson on the right of the line on Missionary ridge. Early on Tuesday morning, the 24th, the pickets at passes of the mountain were reinforced, and at twelve, M., in obedience to my order from the Major General commanding, I sent Pettus' brigade, except the twenty-third and thirtieth Alabama regiments, to report to Brigadier General Jackson, half way down the mountain, leaving me only half of my own brigade, the twenty-third and thirtieth Alabama, and Corquit's battery of Napoleons. The eighteenth and twentieth regiments, (consolidated,) under the command of Lieutenant Colonel Butler, were disposed at Powell's and Nichojack's trails and the contiguous passes. Powell's trail is seven and Nichojack's ten miles from the north point of Lookout. The pass at the point over those nearest to it for two and a half miles on the west side, were held by detachments from the twenty-third and thirtieth Alabama regiments, while reserves from the same regiments, under command of Lieutenant Colonel Hundley, officer of the day, were held near the line of defences south of Summertown to reinforce the pickets. One section of the battery, under charge of ————, was in position near the point, while the other section was held disposable between the point and the line of defences on the south. About half-past twelve, P. M., I moved the thirty-second Tennessee, the largest regiment of my brigade, to reinforce the point and to support the battery. At ten o'clock, P. M., the two Napoleon guns on the point opened fire upon the enemy then passing near the Craven house, and continued it incessantly for two hours. At the same time, I deployed sharpshooters from the thirty-second Tennessee and the thirtieth Alabama down the sides of the mountain and directed a fire upon the enemy's flank. I ordered rocks rolled down the mountain also. The fog was so dense that we could not see the enemy, although we could hear his march, and, guided by this and the report of his musketry, our fire was directed. His advance was quickly checked and his fire materially abated, and doubtless the effect of the shells from the two Napoleon guns and the fire of our sharpshooters contributed largely to this end. Late in the afternoon (the hour not recollected) I reported to the Major General commanding, in answer to a summons from him, and was informed that he had been directed by General Bragg to withdraw from the mountain. I gave orders to all the troops to be ready to move at seven, P. M. Nearly all of our wagons had been ordered the night previous to Chickamauga s'ation for supplies and had not returned. The consequence was that our camp equipage and part of our baggage was abandoned. At seven, P. M., the troops, artillery and ordnance trains were quietly withdrawn to the valley by the Chattanooga road and crossed Chattanooga creek by ten o'clock. The eighteenth and twentieth Tennessee regiments were withdrawn by the McCullough road, and crossed the valley and Missionary ridge by way of Rossville and did not form a junction with the command until late the afternoon of the next day. I halted my brigade on the east side of the Chattanooga creek fronting on that stream, my right resting on the left of Breckinridge's line. At four, A. M., the 25th, I received orders from Major Clare, of General Bragg's staff, to move to the extreme right of the line, which I did at once, reaching the position of Major General Cleburne immediately after sunset. Under the direction of Major General Stevenson, I formed with my left resting over the tunnel through which the East Tennessee and Virginia railroad passes Missionary ridge. My line was soon afterwards changed by Lieutenant General Hardee so as to be in position to support Cleburne's left, or hold the railroad, as occasion might demand. My skirmishers covered the ground from Cleburne's left to the railroad, moving as far forward as Glass station. An hour or two later, by direction of Major General Stevenson, I moved up so as to occupy the interval between the left of Cleburne's line of defence and the railroad. Prolonging Cleburne's line to the railroad, my left considerably advanced. I occupied this position till near sunset. My skirmishers were all the while engaged, and so hotly for a time that I reinforced the line until nearly all my command were deployed as skirmishers. They checked the enemy and prevented his advance, killed and wounded many and captured fifty prisoners. I did not advance from my position because my orders left me no discretion. Indeed, there was probably no time when it would have been advisable. About three o'clock, P. M., Major General Cleburne suggested to me that I might change my front forward on my right battalion and attack the column of the enemy in flank, which was moving immediately on his front. I told him I had just returned from my line of skirmishers, who were hotly engaged, and if I changed the direction of my line I would be exposed to a terrible fire on my flank from the enemy, who was lying under the hill not more than three hundred yards in my front. He readily saw that the movement would be hazardous, and directed me not to make it, but to retain my position. About one hour before sunset I was ordered to move rapidly towards the centre and report to Major General

Cheatham with my command. By this officer's directions, I formed on the left of the remnant of Walthall's brigade, which had its right resting on the line of defence, the enemy having previously penetrated the centre of our line on Missionary ridge. There was an irregular line in our front, skirmishing with the enemy, but it soon retired in broken fragments, and we then advanced. I had orders to conform the movements of my part of the line to that of the command on my right. Before advancing one hundred yards the troops on my right gave way in great disorder, and while that portion was being reformed, orders arrived for me to move by the left flank across to Chickamauga by way of the railroad bridge. Major General Cheatham conducted the movement, and in less than three hours we had effected the crossing near the Shallow ford road.

My entire command, without an exception, behaved well. Captain Tucker, thirty-second Tennessee regiment, had charge of the line of skirmishers on the 25th, and deserves the highest praise for his skill and coolness. I am under renewed obligations to Captain H. J. Cheney, assistant adjutant general, J. T. Brown, first lieutenant and aid-de-camp, Captain J. B. Moore, assistant inspector general of my staff, and M. H. Carter and Geo B. McCullum, acting staff officers, for the prompt and efficient discharge of their respective duties.

Attention is invited to the reports of the regimental commanders herewith filed, respectively, A, B, C, D, and E.

I have the honor to be, Major,

Most respectfully, your obedient servant,
J. W. BROWN,
Brigadier General.

4

REPORT OF BRIGDIER GENERAL PETTUS.

HEADQUARTERS PETTUS' BRIGADE,
Camp near Dalton, Georgia, Dec. 6th, 1863.

Major INGRAM, *Assistant Adjutant General:*

SIR : At half past twelve o'clock, on the 24th ult., I was with my command on the top of Lookout mountain, and was then ordered by Brigadier General Brown, commanding Stevenson's division, to report, with three regiments of my command, to Brigadier General Jackson, commanding at the Craven house. I moved at once with the twentieth, thirty-first and forty-sixth Alabama regiments, and at the head of the column. I found Brigadier General Jackson at the point where the road to the Craven house leaves the road leading down the mountain. Communicating my orders, I was directed to hasten forward, and reinforce Brigadier General Moore, at the Craven house.

On the way, I met squads of Moore's and Walthall's brigades, and, when about three hundred yards from the Craven house, I found that that point had been carried by the enemy. The two brigades which had held the point had fallen back. Here I found Brigadier General Walthall, with the remnant of his command, formed at right angles with, and on the left of the road, gallantly fighting to stay the advance of the enemy. He informed me that he had lost a large part of his command, that his ammunition was nearly exhausted, and that he could not hold the position he then had. Having no time to send back for orders, and finding the fighting was then all on the left of the road, I moved my command, though right in front, by filing to the left, directly up the mountain side, to the rock bluff. As soon as formed, my command was faced by the rear rank, moved forward, relieving Walthall's brigade, and was at once engaged with the enemy. Whilst my command was moving into position, I sent an officer to the right, to find Brigadier General Moore, and to ascertain his condition and the position of his line. In this way I learned that Moore's left was about one hundred and fifty yards from my right, and his right resting at the large rocks in the road, above the mouth of Chattanooga creek. I then went down to Moore's line, and had a few moments consultation with him, and, at his request, extended intervals to the right, so as to connect with his line.

The facts were communicated by me to Brigadier General Jackson, with the request that he would come forward, look at the line, and give us orders ; but he did not come in person, but sent orders that the position must be held. Meantime, the enemy made repeated assaults on my left, next to the bluff, but were bravely met and repulsed by the twentieth Alabama regiment and four companies of the thirty-first Alabama regiment.

Knowing that Brigadier General Moore's line was weak, and knowing that his men were almost out of ammunition, I again sent Captain Smith, of my staff, to inform the Brigadier General commanding as to the progress of the fight, and to ask his assistance. Captain Smith found Brigadier General Jackson at the headquarters of Major General Stevenson, on the top of the mountain, who was then commanding the forces west of Chattanooga creek, about one mile and a half from the fight, where General Jackson informs me he had gone to confer with General Stevenson as to the mode in which the troops should be withdrawn in case the enemy should get possession of the mountain road. In answer to my communication, I was directed to hold my position as long as possible. When I had to send again to the Brigadier General commanding, he was still on the top of the mountain.

After my command had been engaged about two hours, Brigadier General Walthall having formed the remnant of his brigade and supplied his men with ammunition, returned with his command into the fight on the left, and our commands fought together from that time until relieved.

It should be remarked that, during the day, the fog was very dense on the mountain side; it was almost impossible to distinguish any object at the distance of one hundred yards. The enemy made no attack on my right nor on Brigadier General Moore's line; but the attack on the left was continued, and finding that the purpose of the enemy was to force my left, at the suggestion of Brigadier General Walthall, I ordered Captain Davis, commanding the twentieth Alabama regiment, to move forward, keeping his left well up to the bluff, and drive the enemy from the higher ground they then held. The order was executed promptly and in gallant style. The higher ground was gained and held during the fight.

About eight o'clock at night, Clayton's brigade, commanded by Colonel Holtzclaw, relieved Walthall's brigade and the twentieth and thirty-first Alabama regiments, of my command. These two regiments were withdrawn, and formed in the road a short distance in the rear. Sometime after this, I went to the road leading down the mountain, and there met Brigadier General Jackson coming down. He directed me to keep my command where it was and await orders, and then passed on down the mountain. After one o'clock that night, I received orders from the Brigadier General commanding, to retire with my command across Chattanooga creek at the upper bridge, which was done quietly and in good order.

Captains Jones and Smith, of my staff, bore themselves gallantly throughout the affair.

Below is a statement of the casualties in my command. It is small. The day was dark and the men well sheltered in the rocks.

I am, sir, most respectfully,
Your obedient servant,
E. W. PETTUS,
Brigadier General commanding.

CASUALTIES in Pettus' Brigade, in the fight of 24th ultimo:

Killed, 9; wounded, 38; missing, 9. Total loss 56.

REPORT OF BRIGADIER GENERAL MOORE.

HEADQUARTERS MOORE'S BRIGADE, CHEATHAM'S DIVISION,
Near Dalton, Ga., Dec. 3, 1863.

Major JOHN INGRAM,
Assistant Adjutant General:

MAJOR : I have the honor to submit the following report of the part taken by this brigade in the engagement on Lookout mountain, on the 24th, and that on Missionary ridge, on the 25th ultimo :

The brigade was composed of the thirty-seventh Alabama, Lieutenant Colonel Green commanding, the fortieth Alabama, Colonel Higley, and the forty-second Alabama, Lieutenant Colonel Lanier. The result of the engagement on the mountain, as I conceive, renders it necessary for me to enter more fully into details than I would otherwise do.

This position was occupied by my brigade on the right, and Walthall's on the left, or beyond the Craven house, the whole force being under the command of Brigadier General J. K. Jackson. My brigade had charge of the picket line from the mouth of Cattanooga creek to the railroad crossing of Lookout creek, and Walthall's, from that point around to the left.

A few days previous to the attack, I made a reconnoissance of the whole picket line, and forwarded a report, by order of Lieutenant General Hardee, through Brigadier General Jackson. At this time the picket line on Lookout creek extended up that stream about two miles, to a good ford, near an old mill. Our line thus being very long, requiring a large detail (seven hundred) from our comparatively small force, I advised, in my report, the shortening of the line by turning up the mountain at a point known as the Surry house, and that the ford at the old mill be watched by scouting parties during the day and videttes at night. A day or two after this, General Walthall informed me that he had been instructed to picket along the creek only as far as the railroad bridge, extending his line from that point up the mountain. This threw our picket line very near the brigade on the left, rendering them very liable to a surprise, by the enemy crossing above and coming down on the left. Whether this was the case on the day of the assault, I am not sufficiently informed to state, though the result seems to indicate such to have been the case. Up to the time of the assault, none of the enemy had crossed in front of my picket line, and those who escaped inform me that the first intimation they had of the presence of the enemy, on the south side of the creek, was their appearance in force on the side of the mountain in their rear. Consequently the greater portion of the picket force of this brigade (two hundred and twenty-five) were captured.

About eleven o'clock, on the morning of the 24th, I learned the enemy were forming their forces in line of battle in front of our pickets. I went immediately to a point beyond the Craven house, from which I could see that such was the case, and reported the fact in a note to Brigadier General Jackson, informing him also they had commenced skirmishing with our pickets. I ordered my brigade at once under arms, ready to move where ordered. General Jackson ordered me, through a staff officer, to place my brigade in the trenches, on the right of Walthall's. General Walthall's brigade not being in position in the trenches, I informed him of my order, and asked him where his right would rest. I could get no definite answer; he merely stating that he intended to fight first beyond the entrenchments and then falling back, if he found it necessary to do so, and desired that I leave vacant, on the left, space for his command. One of General Jackson's staff being present, told me to wait until he could see the General, and get further or more definite instructions. But the firing on the left in a few moments becoming quite heavy, I thought it advisable to place my command in position without further orders. I at once moved the brigade, urging upon the commanders the importance of dispatch; but, to my utter astonishment, before we reached the trenches (a distance of three or four hundred yards) the enemy had driven back Walthall's brigade, south of the Craven house, and had even occupied a portion of the trenches of my brigade, from which we very soon drove them, on our arrival. We were thus compelled to enter the entrenchments under the fire of the enemy in front, and a very heavy fire from the Moccasin Point batteries, within short range. As Walthall's brigade, where driven back, did not occupy the line on our left, or at least the portion near the Craven house which we could see, the enemy got possession of that position, and also the commanding ground near the house, from which they completely enfiladed my left, which was afterwards retired a little to the right, under cover of the rising ground. We held the position from this time until between three and four o'clock, the enemy repeatedly charging, but repulsed, two of their color-bearers being shot down by our men in the trenches, while attempting to plant their colors on the embankment.

I have never before seen them fight with such daring and desperation. Though they got possession of the Craven house at an early hour, yet they did not attempt to turn the left flank until between three and four o'clock, P. M. We had now been engaged near three hours. We had but thirty rounds of ammunition at first, that being the capacity of the cartridge boxes issued to the brigade, and this supply was now nearly exhausted; entirely so with some of the men. I had not seen Brigadier General Jackson during the day. He gave me no orders during the engagement. I sent a staff officer to his headquarters to inform him of our condition, but he returned and reported he could not find General Jackson, who was absent.

If we had been properly supported on the left, I believe we could have held the trenches even with empty guns. But that support was not given us.

The enemy gradually pressed around my left with an increasing force. I reluctantly gave the order to fall back. We retired about three hundred yards without any great confusion. We here found

Pettus' brigade in line of battle, the prolongation of which line we had selected for a second position. Had General Jackson informed me that his brigade was coming to our support, and had thrown it forward to the trenches on our left, I am confident there would have been no necessity for withdrawing my command from the first position, as this would have prevented our being flanked, or could have driven back the enemy from the left. Had General Jackson been on the ground and given proper orders for the disposition of his command, I feel assured the result would have been very different. The second line we held until about two o'clock, A. M., the 25th, when we were ordered to fall back south of Chattanooga creek.

Our position on Missionary Ridge, on the 25th, was between Walthall's brigade on our right and Jackson's on the left. After the enemy broke our centre, Jackson's brigade was placed perpendicular to the former line to prevent the enemy from sweeping along the line to the right. General Cheatham ordered me to march my brigade by the flank, in rear of and to the left of Jackson's, so as to cover the base of the ridge, and support that brigade. While executing this order, and just as our leading files passed the left of Jackson's brigade, that brigade gave way, rushing back through the ranks of mine, which was still marching by the flank. After stopping them and restoring some order, the two brigades fought as one, both officers and men, though we had at first great difficulty in holding them in line. I did not see General Jackson or any of his staff whom I recognized, except Captain Marino, during the engagement.

The enemy made great efforts to drive us from the position, but failed. We determined to hold it at all hazards, believing that the safety of the right wing of the army, in some measure, and particularly the artillery, depended on our holding this position, which covered one of the roads leading to Chickamauga. We held the line until nearly dark, when I observed the right falling back, and, on inquiring the cause, was informed that an order had been passed down the line from Lieutenant General Hardee to fall back. As a general thing the officers and men of the brigade acted well. I observed Colonel Wilkerson, of the eighth Mississippi, and Lieutenant Colonel Edwards, of the forty-seventh Georgia, of Jackson's brigade, who acted with marked gallantry. Others conducted themselves well, whom I did not recognize.

My own command acted much better than might have been expected under the circumstances, as they fought during the engagements of the two days with arms that had been condemned as unfit for service, and which were received while at Demopolis, Ala., to be used only for drill and guard duty.

I am, Major, very respectfully, your obedient servant,
JOHN C. MOORE,
Brigadier General commanding.

REPORT OF BRIGADIER GENERAL JACKSON.

Headquarters Cheatham's Division,
Near Dalton, Georgia, December 21, 1863.

Major J. J. Reeve,
Assistant Adjutant General:

Major: My report of the unfortunate disaster on Lookout mountain, on the 24th ultimo, has been somewhat delayed in consequence of the delay of the brigade commanders in sending their reports to me; the last of which, that of Brigadier General Moore, was received this day. The result of that day's operations and the character of the reports of brigade commanders, which are herewith enclosed, require of me a report more in detail than I would otherwise make it, and will excuse the personal cast which it assumes.

On the 9th November, 1863, in conformity with orders from army headquarters, being temporarily in command of Cheatham's division, I reported to Major General W. H. F. Walker. A reorganization of the army having just taken place, I had with me, to report to General Walker, but one brigade of the division, Wright's brigade having been left at Charleston, Tenn., under orders, and Moore's and Walthall's brigades having not then reported to me under the new organization. My headquarters were located on the west side of Chattanooga creek, at a point advised by General Walker, and my brigade was placed where he directed. On the same day I was invited by General Walker to accompany him and Lieutenant General Hardee to the Craven's house, which I did. The ground in that neighborhood was passed over, viewed and discussed, but no line to fight on was recommended by any one present. Indeed, it was agreed on all hands, that the position was one extremely difficult of defence against a strong force of the enemy advancing under cover of a heavy artillery fire.

General Walker's opinion was expressed to the effect that, at a certain point to which we had walked, which was a narrow pass, artillery should be placed in position, extending to the left, for a short distance towards the top of the mountain; that this would prevent any surprise by forces approaching in that direction, and, at the same time, they would answer the guns from the hills on the opposite side of Lookout creek: also to have artillery near the Craven house to answer the Moccasin battery guns. By the first arrangement, he said the artillery could have retreated by the roads, and the infantry which was put there to defend the artillery and pass would have felt strong, and been better satisfied and better able to hold their position.

He said his experience was that infantry care but little for artillery if they have artillery to respond with, and that they are soon demoralized when they have quietly to sit and receive artillery fire, without having some of their own to reply with. I ventured to express my own opinion to Lieutenant General Hardee subsequently, and in it I differed somewhat, not without great presumption, but with equal diffidence, from that of so experienced a soldier as General Walker. If we were defeated on the slope, the guns, as I thought, must inevitably be lost from the impossibility of removing them, under fire, from their positions. My plan of defence was to place a gun in every available position on Lookout point, and to sink the wheels or elevate the trails, so as to command the slope of the mountains; in addition to which I respectfully suggested that, on the point, a sharpshooter should be placed wherever a man could stand, so as to annoy the flank of the enemy. In my judgment, there was no place northwest of the Craven house, at which our infantry force could be held on the slope of the mountain, and, in consequence of this firm conviction, I gave orders to Brigadier General Walthall, which are hereinafter mentioned.

Upon my return to the foot of the mountain, on the 9th November, I found Brigadier General Walthall and his brigade in camp there. Brig. General Moore's brigade was then at the Craven house, where it had been for a time; how long I am not informed. General Walker directed that Brigadier General Gist, commanding his division, and I, with my own and Walthall's brigades, of Cheatham's division, should defend the line from Chattanooga creek to the foot of the mountain, and permitted us to divide the line, according to our respective strength, as we wished.

After riding along the line with General Gist, we made the apportionment of it and gave orders to our respective commands. At that time, I had no command over the mountain slope, although one of my brigades (Moore's) of the division was then on duty at or near the Craven house. General Moore was in command of that portion of the line, under General Walker's orders, from 10th to 14th November. The command I found General Walker exercising, extended over all the troops west of Chattanooga creek, under the general supervision of Lieutenant General Hardee, and upon General Walker going away, on a short leave, on the 12th November, which he informed me he had some weeks before applied for, and upon the assurance of General Bragg that he would telegraph him when Sherman came up, before which time he anticipated no trouble, this command devolved on me. I at once asked for written instructions from the corps commander as to the mode of defence of the line, but received none. The command was a unit, and was doubtless intended to be handled as such. I continued to exercise it, and gave orders, subject to the approval of Lieutenant General Hardee, until his headquarters were removed from the extreme right of the army to a point a little east of Chattanooga creek. This was about the 14th November.

About this time, I went to the top of the mountain with Lieutenant General Hardee. We there met General Bragg, and after a view from Lookout point, General Bragg indicated a line on the slope of the mountain, which, from that stand-point, he thought ought to be the fighting line. As we descended the mountain, I again rode out with Lieutenant General Hardee to the Craven house, and again looked over the ground. The line indicated by General Bragg, was found to present quite a different appearance, upon a close view, from the same as seen from the mountain top. This line, as I understood it, passed from Lookout point, a little in rear of the Craven house, and down to a point not far from the junction of the Kelly's ferry and Craven house roads, and thence to the precipitous rocks near the mouth of Chattanooga creek. The engineers were put to work under some one's orders—whose I do not know—and fatigue parties furnished to them from my command, at their request.

On the 14th November, a new disposition of the command was made. Major General Stevenson was assigned to the command of the troops and defences on the top of Lookout mountain The ranking officer of Cheatham's division was directed to assume command of all troops and defences at and near the Craven house. The ranking officer of Walker's division was charged with the line from the base of Lookout mountain east to Chattanooga creek, and all the troops not at the points above named This order emanated from headquarters Hardee's corps, and in conformity with it, as the ranking officer of Cheatham's division, I assumed command of the troops and defences at and near the Craven house, and on the following day (the 15th November) established my headquarters at the junction of the Summertown road with the mountain side road, leading to the Craven house, with the approval of Lieutenant General Hardee. On the same day, Brigadier General Walthall's brigade relieved that of Brigadier General Pettus' near the Craven house.

On the night of the 16th or 17th, a fatigue party was ordered to report to Lieutenant Steele, of the engineers, to commence work on the new line below the Craven house. By direction of Lieutenant General Hardee, I went out, in person, to see that the work was progressing ; found that there was a misunderstanding as to the place of reporting ; walked down the road a considerable distance along the contemplated line ; then went to the Craven house and ordered the detail to reassemble, and to report to Lieutenant Steele immediately. This was at night. The work was directed to be done at night, as the working party would be under the fire of the Moccasin Point batteries.

General Walthall's troops being some distance in advance of the proposed line, and exposed to the enemy's artillery fire, I ordered him, on the 18th, with the approval of Lieutenant General Hardee, to shorten his picket line, as he proposed, and notice of which I promptly gave to General Stevenson, and to bring back his troops in the rear (south) of the Craven house, leaving his picket line where they were, supported by one regiment.

Upon inspection of the ground, General Walthall reported to me that, as General Moore's troops were also in the rear of the Craven house, there would not be room enough for his brigade between General Moore's and my headquarters, and said that, as he supposed the order I had given him was permissive, rather than directory, if I had no objections, he would keep his troops where they were. To this I assented, giving him, at the same time, instructions, if attacked by the enemy in heavy force, to fall back fighting over the rocks. I expected, by the time his troops reached the Craven house, to be with them, and form line of battle with Walthall's left against the cliff, and his right at or near the Craven house, and Moore prolonging this line to the right This was the general line pointed out by General Bragg, although it had not been defined by the engineers, nor had any work been done it between the cliff and the Craven house. Beyond the Craven house there was no practicable line which was not enfiladed by the enemy's batteries, except the covered way prepared by General Jenkins, and the flank of that was exposed to the infantry attack On the afternoon of the 20th, (I believe,) I visited the works below the Craven house, in company with Captain Henry, of the division staff, and spent some time in their inspection. These works being a mere rifle pit, would be of no service when the enemy were once in possession of the Craven house, as they would thence be taken in flank—almost in reverse.

On the 22d November, my own brigade was ordered to report to me, and was moved from the top of the mountain. to the slope and placed in the position which I had desired General Walthall to take. On the 23d, it was ordered to the foot of the mountain, out of my command, to take, with Cumming's brigade, the place on the line which had been occupied by Walker's division—my position and that of General Stevenson—and thus each were weakened by a brigade. On the same day a brisk fire of artillery and small arms was heard, coming from the extreme right. It was supposed to be a struggle for wood. Late in the afternoon of the 23d, General Stevenson was placed in command of the forces west of Chattanooga creek, Lieutenant General Hardee having been removed to the extreme right, and on the same night orders were received and distributed to prepare three days' cooked rations, and to hold the troops in readiness to move at a moment's notice. In order to avoid anything like a suprise along the line, at about half-past seven o'clock, P M., I ordered Captain Henry, of the division staff, to visit the "chiefs of pickets," and direct them to be unusually vigilant in watching the movements of the enemy and to guard against surprise.

About nine o'clock, A. M., of the 24th, I received a note from General Walthall to the effect that the enemy were moving in heavy force towards our left; that their tents had nearly all disappeared and their pontoon bridges been cut away. Shortly afterwards, I received another note from him, to the effect that he was mistaken as to the number of tents that had disappeared, but that many of those which could be seen on previous days were not then visible. The originals of both these notes were immediately dispatched to General Bragg, and copies to General Stevenson. I also sent a staff officer to order Generals Moore and Walthall to hold their commands under arms, ready for action. I walked out on the road towards the Craven house, to a favorable point, and could distinguish the enemy's troops in the plain in front of Chattanooga; all quiet; no massing; no movements of any kind. From this point I sent another staff officer to the Craven house, to report to me, immediately, anything of interest, and returned myself to my position at the fork of the road. The demonstrations of the enemy did not, down to this time, indicate the point of attack, whether upon my portion of the line, or further to the left. General

Stevenson inquired of me about this time, if I needed reinforcements, to which I replied, that I could not tell until there were further developments. I sent orders, by a staff officer, to Generals Moore and Walthall, to place their troops in line as soon as skirmishing commenced, but not unnecessarily to expose them to the fire of the enemy's artillery. I expected, from the rugged nature of the ground, and the fact that the enemy had to ascend the mountain, that the picket fighting would continue for some time before the main body would be engaged. About this time I received a message from Gen. Moore, that he did not know where the line was. I sent back immediately an order that General Walthall would occupy the left, and that he (General Moore,) would form on General Walthall's right, prolonging the line in the earthworks below the Craven house, as far as his troops would extend. About twelve, M., I received a note from General Moore, that the enemy had formed line and commenced skirmishing with our pickets near the railroad bridge, crossing Lookout creek; that he could not then tell their object, and enquiring where he should place his brigade. I sent to General Stevenson to ask for the offered reinforcements.

Information came to me from General Walthall, about the same time, that the pickets had commenced firing, and a message from Gen. Stevenson, by Major Pickett, that the enemy was making an attack on my line. I now asked, in writing, for a brigade from General Stevenson, to be sent down at once, and ordered Major John Ingram, assistant adjutant general, to direct General Walthall to fight back the enemy with his pickets and reserves as long as possible, and finally to take position with his left against the cliff, and his right at or in direction of the Craven house, and to direct General Moore to advance and form on the right of General Walthall, and prolong the line in the earthworks below the Craven house, passing General Moore's brigade moving up to their position, and to support General Walthall's brigade, which was being rapidly driven back by overwhelming numbers.

The substance of my order was delivered by Major Ingram to Generals Moore and Walthall. The latter stated that although the order did not reach him in time, he had carried it out in his efforts to defend the position. General Moore, expressing a desire to have full supply of ammunition, was informed by Major Ingram that Captain Clark, division ordnance officer, had been ordered to furnish him from the division train. Within a few minutes after Major Ingram left, as bearer of the above order to Generals Moore and Walthall, I proceeded in person, accompanied by Major Vaulx, of the division staff, to superintend the execution. Passing a great many stragglers, officers and men, along the road, I was met at some short distance from the Craven house by an officer from General Walthall, who brought the information that his brigade had been driven back in considerable confusion and that the Craven house was in possession of the enemy. I immediately dispatched a staff officer to speed the reinforcements and endeavored to rally the men, who were coming to the rear in large numbers, and form a line, where I was selecting what I considered the most favorable position for a line, among rocks, where no regular line was practicable, and where the battle could be but a general skirmish. Failing in this, I rode back to the junction of the roads, and there met Brigadier General Pettus, with three regiments of his brigade. He informed me that he had been ordered by General Stevenson to report to me. I directed him to proceed on the road and form line to reinforce Generals Moore and Walthall. I at the same time sent for a piece of artillery from the battalion of the division, and upon its arrival, directed the officer in command to select the most favorable position on the Craven house road and check the enemy. He soon after reported that he could find no position in which he could use his gun to advantage, and for not more than one or two shots at all. I remained generally at the junction of the two roads, because I considered it most accessible from all points. General Stevenson was communicating with me by the road down the mountain, and Generals Pettus and Walthall by the crossroad. General Pettus informed me, by an officer, of the disposition made of his troops, and asked for orders. Having placed his regiments on the left of the cross-road, with their left against the cliff, and extended intervals so as to connect with General Moore on the right of the road, I had no orders to give him except to hold that position against the enemy. His dispositions were satisfactory, and I did not wish to change them. I subsequently received a message from him, that the enemy was pressing his left and asking for reinforcements, and at the same time I was informed by one of the division staff that General Walthall had sent the fragments of two regiments to that point and there was no danger to be apprehended there. I replied to General Pettus that I had no reinforcements to send him; that no more could be obtained from General Stevenson, and he must hold his position.

The enemy being held in check, matters so continued, not materially changed, until quite late in the afternoon, when I received a report, by an officer of General Moore's brigade, that unless he was reinforced his right would be turned. Receiving intelligence also from officers of pickets, who had escaped that way, that the Kelley's Ferry road was entirely open, I knew that the enemy had only to press forward on it to obtain control of our road from the mountain; and, expecting that they would certainly do so, I rode to the top of the mountain to confer with General Stevenson, my immediate superior, upon the subject. We agreed that if the enemy did get possession of the road at or near the base of the mountain, I should withdraw the troops of my command at dark, and join him on the top of the mountain, and he so directed. Availing myself of General Stevenson's writing material, I addressed written orders to the division quartermaster, commissary, ordnance officer and chief of artillery, who were in the plain below, to retire beyond Chattanooga creek, and then look for orders from corps headquarters, as I expected to be cut off from them. After this short absence, I returned to my position on the mountain side, and there remained until near dark, having sent orders to the brigade commanders that if we were cut off or overpowered, we would retire by the top of the mountain, but to hold their positions, if possible, until dark, and to await further orders. When it was near dark, and when the firing had become rather desultory, I again went to General Stevenson's headquarters for final orders as to withdrawing the troops. I was there informed that General Bragg ordered us to retire down the mountain—the road being still open—and that we must assemble at the Gillespie house, to make final arrangements.

A guard having been detailed from my command for some subsistence stores on the top of the mountain, I went to relieve them, but found that it had already been done. Proceeding to the Gillespie house, at the base of the mountain, I received orders from General Bragg, through General Cheatham, as to the time and mode of withdrawing the troops, and immediately dispatched them to the brigade commanders by the assistant adjutant general and the acting inspector general of the division. In conformity with these orders, the troops retired south of Chattanooga creek, and the bridge was destroyed.

On the 20th of November, the date of the report nearest to the day of the battle, Moore's brigade had a total effective of one thousand two hundred and five, and Walthall's brigade a total effective of one thousand four hundred and eighty-nine. The casualties in the first were four killed, forty-eight wounded and one hundred and ninety-nine missing. In the second, the casualties were eight killed, ninety-one wounded and eight hundred and forty-five captured. In Pettus' brigade there were nine killed, thirty-eight wounded and nine missing.

General Moore ventures the opinion that if I had given proper orders a different result would have been accomplished I beg leave to differ. The whole effective force at my command, at the beginning, was twenty-six hundred and ninety-four men. Of these, one thousand and forty-four had been captured, some had been wounded, and a few killed. The enemy's force was (as reported) a division and two brigades. They were in possession of the high grounds around the Craven house, from which, by General Moore's own statement, his left was completely enfiladed. Under these circumstances, I was unwilling to hazard an advance movement with my shattered command, though aided by the three regiments under General Pettus, who was himself pressed by the enemy. General Moore adds a report of the battle the next day on Missionary ridge, when he was not under my command, and goes out of his way to say that he did not see me during the engagement. I did not think it necessary for me to show myself to him. If he had desired to see me, he could have found me at *all* times during the engagement near the right of my line, which was on the top of the ridge, while the left was down the hill. If General Moore means to reflect upon the conduct of my brigade, I am glad to say that there are other witnesses who bear different testimony.

General Walthall must have misapprehended the remark made to him as I descended the mountain. I expected to receive orders from General Bragg, but not to see him in person. These orders were to come through General Cheatham.

It may be remarked that there were two six-pounder guns at the

Craven house, under the command of Lieutenant Gibson, but they were without horses, and could not be moved. In their position they could not be fired without endangering the troops of General Walthall. Lieutenant Gibson's report accompanies this. He never reported to me, although subject to my orders; and his two guns were all the artillery that I could command for purposes of defence, although I took the responsibility of ordering up a piece from the battalion of Cheatham's division.

General Walthall's communication, in relation to a piece of artillery to be placed in position, was sent by me, immediately on its receipt, to General Stevenson. Captain Henry, of the division staff, was the bearer of it.

The movements of the enemy were very rapid. An impenetrable fog hung around the mountain all day.

I am, Major, very respectfully,
Your obedient servant,
JOHN K. JACKSON,
Brigadier General.

ENGAGEMENT AT KNOXVILLE.

REPORT OF LIEUTENANT COLONEL M. A. HAYNES.

DEPARTMENT OF EAST TENNESSEE, }
Knoxville, June 21, 1863. }

To Major VON SHILIHA,
  Acting Chief of Staff:

SIR: At the request of Colonel Trigg, temporarily in command of the troops at Knoxville, (in the absence of Major General Buckner,) I have the honor to report to you the following particulars in regard to the battle of yesterday:

On the 18th instant, I returned to this city from Sevier, where I had been in command of an expedition against a party of bushwhackers.

On my arrival, I learned that Major General Buckner had marched towards Big Creek gap, with all the artillery and all the other disposable force at this post, except Colonel Trigg's fifty-first Virginia regiment and Colonel Finley's seventh Florida regiment, effective force about one thousand men.

On the morning of the 19th I was informed by Major Von Shiliha, acting chief of staff, that the enemy, in large force, had passed by London, and were at Lenoir station, twenty-four miles from Knoxville, and he requested me to take charge of the artillery defence of the city and to organize my force from the convalescents in the hospitals and from citizens, to man my guns then in the city. At the same time he gave the following order:

"HEADQUARTERS DEPARTMENT EAST TENNESSEE, }
"*June* 19, 1863. }

"Major Reynolds, chief of ordnance, will issue to Lieutenant Colonel Haynes' corps artillery, C. S. A., as many field pieces as can possibly be put in condition within a few hours.

"He also will furnish Lieutenant Colonel Haynes with all necessary equipments, and with one hundred rounds of ammunition.

"By order of Major General Buckner.
   "J. VON SHILIHA, *Chief of Staff.*"

In obedience to this order, (given to me in the absence of General Buckner,) I went to the ordnance department and found eight pieces of field artillery there, but no harness. Major Reynolds promptly said that in one hour he would have the ammunition chests filled, and that they would be subject to my orders.

I then went to Major Glover, chief quartermaster of East Tennessee, and requested him to send to the ordnance department seventy horses or mules with harness, and drivers for every two.

In the meantime, the citizens of Knoxville had been ordered to report to me or to Colonel Blake for duty, for the defence of the city.

Finding myself too much engaged to obey this order in person, I appointed Major H. Baker (formerly of the artillery of Tennessee) to receive and assign them to duty as they reported.

At three in the afternoon of that day, it was known that the enemy was within five miles of the city, and their advance were skirmishing with thirty-seven of our cavalry men, all we had at Knoxville, at Mrs. Lemis' house.

At this hour, Major Glover had already sent the requisite number of horses, mules and drivers for the eight pieces of artillery at the ordnance department. I immediately posted them in sections at College hill, under Major Baker, (the exposed point,) second on McGee's hill, under Captain Hugh L. W. McClung, and third, under Lieutenant Patterson and Lieutenant J. J. Burroughs, at Summit hill, in front of the ordnance department. This last battery had been fortified during the afternoon, under the superintendence of Captain Foster, of the engineers, (by my order,) with a cotton bale revetment, the cotton bales having been promptly sent from all quarters by Major Glover, chief quartermaster.

During that evening, the enemy failing to advance, Colonel Trigg, (temporarily in command at Knoxville,) without consulting me, removed Major Baker's battery from College hill to a point near the Asylum hospital.

In the evening, upon hearing the reports of my officers, I ascertained that about two hundred persons, citizens, and convalescent soldiers from hospitals, had reported for duty, and that each of my batteries was fully manned, although, in the morning of the same day, there was no artillery force whatever in the city.

During the night I made a reconnoissance, passing through the enemy's lines as a farmer, giving all the information they desired in regard to the state of the defences; telling them that they could march into Knoxville without the loss of a man. I told them that I saw Colonel Haynes about sunset moving some cannon towards the depot; I thought about four in all, drawn by mules.

Having passed to a point at which it was necessary for me to turn off, and having all the information I could obtain, I returned to Knoxville at midnight. I visited all my batteries, and advised them that early in the morning the enemy would attack, and directed Captain McClung and Major Baker to consider themselves as reserved, to be moved whenever needed.

During the night, the pickets of the enemy advanced upon the city, but our pickets, thrown out by Colonel Trigg, after an hour's skirmish, drove them back at about two o'clock in the morning. At seven o'clock, on the 20th, four pieces of artillery, detached by General Buckner from his command, reached the ordnance depot, (where I then was,) and I immediately conducted them to the rear as a reserve. I then went to Summit Hill battery, where I found Colonel Trigg and his chief of staff, Major Shiliha, near the hospital. While in consultation with them, we saw the enemy march at double quick time on our right, beyond the work-shops, where we had neither battery nor soldiers to oppose them. Colonel Trigg soon afterwards ordered Colonel Finley's seventh regiment Florida volunteers, and two pieces of Wyley's battery, to take possession of Temperance hill, but before this order was given I had taken a section of Wyley's battery, and moved them at a gallop to a point immediately in front of the advancing column, and opened fire upon them with spherical case. The enemy took shelter behind houses and fences, and threw forward sharpshooters within two hundred yards of our battery—we being entirely unsupported by infantry, and four hundred yards from any support.

At the same time, a battery of three-inch rifle guns, belonging to the enemy, opened upon us at eight hundred yards, and, during the first two or three shots, killed and wounded some of our men and several horses. I then advanced the battery, and ordered them not to fire at the artillery, but at the infantry.

The enemy, at this moment, forming column, advanced rapidly, and, for a moment, I supposed the day was lost. At this moment, the chief of the twelfth howitzer said to me, " Colonel, I can't hit them fellows; please get down and try it yourself." I dismounted, took my post as a gunner to the left, ordered canister and sighted the piece myself, and, after two rounds, the enemy was in full retreat, and the day was won.

During the same time, the battery under Lieutenant J. J. Burroughs and Lieutenant Patterson, on Summit hill, was also engaged, and kept up a continual fire, during which Captain McClung and Lieutenant Fellows were killed.

The section under Lieutenant Whelon having reached Temperance hill, opened fire upon the retreating enemy, which, with the fire from Wyley's battery, Burroughs' battery, and Major Baker's completed the victory.

During the fight, although sharpshooters were sent out against us, none were sent out to sustain us, although one thousand men were immediately behind us.

The enemy had one battery of artillery, and about two thousand six hundred men, opposed to about one thousand men, part of whom were citizens and convalescent soldiers. That they were fully beaten may appear from the fact that the commanding officer of the enemy sent to me a message, (by Lieutenant Lutrell, of the Confederate States army, a prisoner paroled by him,) to the effect, " I send you my compliments, and say that, but for the admirable manner with which you managed your artillery, I would have taken Knoxville to-day."

It is not out of place for me to say that Colonel E. D. Blake, chief of conscripts, and, for the day, commander of all volunteer infantry, contributed, by his zeal and well-known courage, to the honorable result.

Amongst many citizens who reported to me that day for duty, I must not forget to mention Honorable Landon C. Haynes, Honorable W. H. Sneed, Honorable John H. Crozier, Reverend James H. Martin and Reverend Mr. Woolfolk, and many others, who do not desire me to mention their names.

With such compatriots and such fellow-soldiers, I might, willingly, at any time, meet the foe.

I have the honor to be
Your most obedient servant,
MILTON A. HAYNES,
Lt. Col. P. A. C. S., commanding artillery.

ENGAGEMENT

AT

LIMESTONE CREEK.

REPORT OF LIEUTENANT COLONEL M. A. HAYNES.

HEADQUARTERS ARTILLERY,
Fourth District, Department of East Tennessee,
Jonesboro', September 12, 1864.

Captain W. B. REESE,
Assistant Adjutant General:

SIR: In obedience to the orders of the Brigadier General commanding, I have the honor to enclose to you, the reports of Lieutenants Blackwell and Graham, of Burrough's battery, in regard to the engagement with the Federal force, commanded by Colonel Hayes, of the one hundredth Ohio regiment, on the 8th instant.

These officers have detailed the incidents of the 8th so well that I have but little to add.

On the 6th, as you know, our whole force was at Bristol, on which day we marched to Jonesboro', arriving there on the morning of the 7th. The enemy had already been in Jonesboro'; taken away many citizens prisoners and carried them off, and having possession of the trains south of Jonesboro', they told their Union friends (as reported to us) that they would be back on the 8th. Many citizens had been despoiled by the enemy, and my forces were anxious to avenge their wrongs.

At two o'clock, on the morning of the 8th, General Jackson sent me an order requiring me to send immediately forward one piece of artillery. I sent a six-pounder with sixty rounds, and went myself to see them off; but at the General's headquarters I was met by one of his officials who told me I was ordered to remain in charge. I returned to my quarters, and early in the morning, I heard the sound of artillery and then of small arms. An order soon came requiring two companies of infantry, which were sent. About eight o'clock in the morning, a messenger came from General Jackson, saying "send me all your artillery and all the infantry except one company." My artillery was already harnessed and every man at his post, and, at the word, they were on the march, and Lieutenant Colonel Walker's battalion North Carolina volunteers, three hundred strong, followed.

Arriving at Tilford's station, where we had the battle of the morning, we saw our wounded, and heard that the enemy were in retreat, and that General Jackson was in pursuit. Not knowing in what direction friends or foes had gone, we pursued in a gallop, and at about nine o'clock, we heard the discharge of artillery at Limestone bridge.

Pursuing our course as rapidly as possible, we soon came to the scene of action, and placed our pieces in battery. At that moment Colonel Giltner, of the Kentucky cavalry, with his men dismounted, was engaged with the enmy on the opposite side of Limestone creek, cutting off the communication of the enemy, by railroad, south. Soon after, Colonel Walker came up with his men, who had marched at double-quick time twelve miles. At my suggestion, they were ordered to lie down and rest for thirty minutes, and during that time the enemy's sharpshooters were firing upon our battery, and we were amusing them by a few discharges of spherical case shot.

As soon as Colonel Walker's men had rested they deployed as skirmishers to the left, to clear the woods, and Major McCanny's battalion on the right to sustain the battery. At that moment the enemy had possesion of a skirt of woods in front of the blockhouse and stone and brick buildings, occupied by them as barracks, distant about one thousand yards from our position.

The infantry advancing, as arranged, charged the enemy's skirmishers, the battery covering them by throwing case and canister into the woods occupied by them.

With a shout and a hurrah for the "*Bonnie Blue Flag*," the North Carolina boys made the charge and the enemy fled before them, as you and the General well know.

The enemy being now within the blockhouse and other houses, were pouring upon us a shower of minnie balls.

When we had thus driven the enemy into their last retreat, (Colonel Giltner with his gallant Kentuckians accompanying to the other side of the creek,) I brought the guns of Burrough's battery, then under Blackwell, into position and opened fire upon them with spherical case and canister shot, Colonel Giltner's small rifle guns joining in the action. The enemy in the meantime kept up on us a very sharp fire of small arms (enfield,) and then (as Sterne says) a white flag appeared.

By order of General Jackson, I went down, accompanied by Captain Robert B. Haynes, aid-de-camp, and accepted the side arms of near three hundred and fifty Yankee officers and soldiers, the remnant of four hundred and fifty, who began the fight in the morning.

Among the men who, by their gallantry, contributed to the result, were Lieutenant Colonel James Bottles and Captain Jenkins, both volunteers for the occasion, but men whose bravery could not be exceeded.

Our troops, of all arms, behaved with courage, and all within their sphere contributed to the general and honorable result, among whom I ought not to leave out, and do not leave out, the names of the gallant Lieutenant Colonel Wynne, of Georgia, Colonel Giltner, of Kentucky, and among whom, and over all of us, was the gallant commanding General.

I have the honor to be, very respectfully,
Your obedient servant,
MILTON A. HAYNES,
Lieutenant Colonel, P. A. C. S., commanding Artillery.

HEADQUARTERS DEPARTMENT EAST TENNESSEE,
Zollicoffer, Sept. 22, 1863.

Major STANTON, A. A. General:

SIR: In regard to the engagement of yesterday and the day before, on the banks of the Wautauga river, at Carter's station, I have this to report to you, to be submitted to the commanding General:

On the morning of the 19th (General Jackson being in command,) I posted my batteries on the right and left of the depot, upon the heights, and soon afterwards the enemy in front attacked the cavalry under General Crittenden, and for three hours a sharp skirmish was kept up between our forces and the enemy. During this time the enemy pushed forward a battery of three-inch rifled guns (Parrott) and opened upon our batteries; but, by the direction of myself and Colonel King, our batteries never returned their fire.

During this time I rode forward to the scene of the engagement and requested General Crittenden to allow me to bring my guns into the action, but he told me at that moment they would be of no use. Soon after a train arrived from Zollicoffer, bearing General John S. Williams and his brigade, of which was the forty-fifth Virginia, commanded by Colonel Brown.

I immediately went with General Williams to examine the position of our forces, and, by his orders, during that night, I constructed a foot bridge on trestles across the Wautauga river, a half a mile above the railroad bridge in order to effect a communication with our forces who were stationed on the opposite side of the river. In the construction of this bridge I was aided by Colonel Johnson, of Arkansas, and the Hon. Joseph B. Heiskell, member of Congress from Tennessee, both of whom were volunteers for the occasion, and at nine o'clock that night the bridge was completed.

At three in the morning of the 20th, the enemy, having advanced a battery of rifled pieces, opened a spirited fire upon the depot, where there were three trains loaded with quartermaster's and commissary's stores, to be sent to Zollicoffer; but, by order of General Williams, neither our batteries or infantry returned the fire of the enemy. In the morning our cavalry, dismounted, under General Crittenden, advanced upon the enemy, and for some two or three hours skirmished with with them. During this time, two regiments of the enemy having passed, with banners flying and drums beating, under the shelter of a hill, deployed in front of McClung's battery, which was on the south side of the river at about five thousand yards distant, evidently with the intention of storming it; and Captain McClung (although commanded not to fire without my order,) opened upon them with spherical case, and, after about forty rounds, no enemy was to be seen but the dead.

In the afternoon the enemy suddenly displayed a battery of artillery in a point of woods near our position, and then General Williams said, "turn your guns loose," and under the direction of Lieutenant Colonel King, Lowry's battery of Napoleon guns, and Burrough's battery of rifled guns, opened on the enemy's battery, and in about twenty minutes the enemy was no longer to be seen. After dark General Williams ordered me to take three companies of infantry across the river, deploy them as skirmishers, and bring on an action at the setting of the moon. Lieutenant Colonel King, of the artillery was to take charge of Colonel Brown's regiment, which was to support me, by a movement on the right. In obedience to these orders I deployed three companies as skirmishers at eight paces, covering the entire front of the enemy's pickets, and within two hundred yards of them, with orders to open upon the enemy when the moon set, and it was already in the trees when an order came to me by assistant adjutant general Reese, requiring me to withdraw my forces and McClung's battery, and burn the bridge, which order was given to me in the name of Major General Sam Jones, communicated from Zollicoffer by telegraph. This order was obeyed, except I had to abandon the carriages of McClung's battery, bringing off the metal only, and the three companies posted on the hill to the left of McClung's battery, effected their escape by crossing on the trestle bridge, which had been built the night before by order of General Williams. And that night at four o'clock I started with all my guns to Zollicoffer, where I reported to Major General Sam Jones for duty at nine o'clock in the morning.

I have the honor to be,
Very respectfully, your obedient servant,
MILTON A. HAYNES,
Lieutenant Colonel, P. A. C. S., commanding Artillery.

www.ingramcontent.com/pod-product-compliance
Lightning Source LLC
Chambersburg PA
CBHW020240090426
42735CB00010B/1775